"A government's effectiveness, and indeed its very legitimacy, depend on curbing legislative corruption. Pelizzo and Stapenhurst provide much-needed guidance for developed and developing countries alike."

—*Andrew Spalding,* University of Richmond School of Law

"Pelizzo and Stapenhurst continue their productive collaboration on the comparative study of corruption with this analysis of the role played by legislatures in curbing (as well as facilitating) corrupt practices. This book reviews and extends contemporary research on the subject and offers advice for using legislative institutions to improve governance."

—*Thomas Mann,* Brookings Institution

Corruption and Legislatures

This book investigates parliaments' role in curbing corruption. In addition to discussing the definition, causes, and costs of corruption and the role that parliaments have in reducing corruption, the authors consider contemporary issues that parliamentarians—and others—need to be aware of. These include the importance of broad-based coalitions to fight corruption and networking at the country, regional, and global levels; the importance—and difficulties—of establishing parliamentary codes of ethics/conduct; legislative oversight tools and mechanisms; and regional/international conventions against corruption. Attention will also be given to parliaments and anti-money laundering.

Corruption and Legislatures presents a non-technical review of contemporary issues and recent developments in curbing corruption, and concludes with practical advice as to what can be done to ensure more effective parliamentary involvement in curbing corruption.

Riccardo Pelizzo is a consultant to the World Bank Institute.

Frederick Stapenhurst is a Professor of Practice at McGill University and a consultant/advisor to the World Bank Institute.

Routledge Research in Comparative Politics

For a full list of titles in this series, please visit www.routledge.com

Corruption and Legislatures

Riccardo Pelizzo and Frederick Stapenhurst

Routledge
Taylor & Francis Group

LONDON AND NEW YORK

First published 2014 by Routledge

2 Park Square, Milton Park, Abingdon, Oxfordshire OX14 4RN
711 Third Avenue, New York, NY 10017

Routledge is an imprint of the Taylor & Francis Group, an informa business

First issued in paperback 2018

Library of Congress Cataloging-in-Publication Data

Pelizzo, Riccardo.
  Corruption and legislatures / by Riccardo Pelizzo and Frederick
Stapenhurst.
    pages cm — (Routledge research in comparative politics ; 59)
  1. Legislative oversight.   2. Legislative oversight—Moral and
ethical aspects.   3. Political corruption.   4. Political corruption—
Prevention.   5. Political ethics.   6. Comparative government.
I. Stapenhurst, Frederick.   II. Title.
  JF229.P36   2014
  328.3'45—dc23
  2013047611

ISBN: 978-0-415-73010-5 (hbk)
ISBN: 978-1-138-38426-2 (pbk)

Typeset in Sabon
by Apex CoVantage, LLC

Contents

Figures

Tables

1 Introduction

For many years, neither scholars nor practitioners paid sufficient attention to corruption. Corruption was nothing more than an afterthought. It was considered as a byproduct of pre-modern forms of economic organization, the result of inadequate political development and something that could possibly favor development as it could grease the wheels of rigid, incompetent, and excessively bureaucratic public administrations. Scholars paid little attention to the empirical characteristics of corruption, its causes and its consequences, while development practitioners avoided the issue because they considered it as a matter of a country's internal politics, and as such, with no impact whatsoever on development. Legislatures—if considered at all—were usually thought of as being "part of the problem" and little thought was given to how legislatures could help control corruption.

In recent years, two strands of research and practice have proceeded more or less in parallel, with little cross-over, despite apparent synergy. The control of corruption—with corruption defined as ". . . acts in which the power of public office is used for personal gain in a manner that contravenes the rules of the game" (Jain, 2001, p. 73)—has emerged as an important element of governance. There is now a substantial body of literature that demonstrates that *corruption matters*. From early claims that corruption was either a byproduct of development (Naim, 1994), or even the "grease" that actually aided development (Huntington, 1968; Neff, 1964), thinking has rotated 180 degrees and there appears to be consensus that corruption hinders development (Mauro, 1997; Wei and Kaufmann, 1998; Kaufmann, 2000; Drury, Kreikhaus, and Lusztig, 2006; among others). Indeed, reducing it has become a stated goal of many governments.

Legislative oversight has also attracted attention from scholars and practitioners alike, although there is no consensus on what oversight actually is. Some researchers have suggested that it consists of legislative supervision of the policies and programs enacted by government (Schick, 1976), while others extend the definition to include supervision of the executive's proposed legislative programs (e.g., Maffio, 2002). In recent years, attention has focused on the tools that a legislature has to oversee government (Maffio, 2002; Pennings, 2000) and, more recently still, to the relation between legislative oversight tools and types of government (i.e., presidential, semi-presidential, and parliamentary) and degree of democracy (Pelizzo and Stapenhurst, 2004; Pelizzo and Stapenhurst, 2008).

Kaufmann and Dininio (2006), Johnston and Kpundeh (2001) and others have highlighted the fact that multifaceted strategies are required to repress corruption—and one of the key components of such strategies is legislative oversight. However, empirical research on whether this is true, and if it is, *how* oversight curbs corruption has been lacking; this issue has not been studied by either corruption scholars or legislative experts.

In their seminal work, Lederman, Loayza, and Soares (2001, 2005) determined that political institutions are important when it comes to curbing corruption. They found that legislatures in parliamentary systems are more effective in controlling corruption than legislatures in presidential systems. This conclusion has been corroborated by Gerring and Thacker (2004) and Gerring, Thacker, and Moreno (2005) who show that parliamentary forms of government (along with unitarism [Gerring and Thacker, 2004]) and proportional representation (Gerring, Thacker, and Moreno, 2005) help reduce corruption. Kunicova and Rose-Ackerman (2005, 2007) point out that presidentialism (along with proportional representation electoral systems) are associated with higher levels of corruption. Organizations such as the World Bank and Transparency International note the importance of legislative oversight strategies to curb corruption, but, again, they have not analyzed how legislative oversight helps reduce corruption.

The analysis here extends the work of Lederman, Loayza, and Soares (2001, 2005) and Pelizzo and Stapenhurst (2004, 2006, 2008) and confirms that the type of government is a determining factor in addressing corruption. By examining semi-presidential as well as presidential and parliamentary systems, Pelizzo and Stapenhurst demonstrated that the availability of oversight tools to a legislature is a major factor in the latter's success in helping to curb corruption. Still lacking, however, is serious consideration of how the other core functions of a legislature—legislation/policy-making and representation—can contribute to the control of corruption. Also lacking are analyses on how and why legislatures may be part of the problem of corruption, including political party and electoral finance and the lack of sanctioning of unethical behavior by legislators and electoral laws. These gaps are addressed in this book.

This book is divided into four sections. The first comprises an overview of corruption and legislatures, while the second looks at legislatures as both contributing to the solution of corruption and also being part of the problem. The third looks at ways that legislatures can improve their performance; it also presents some conclusions. In the Annex, an overview of how legislatures can help reduce money laundering is presented.

In the rest of this chapter, we present a short overview of corruption—highlighting the types, costs, and causes of corruption and the role that the legislature plays in anti-corruption strategies. In Chapter 2, we examine corruption in greater detail, noting that it is not just a political problem, but also an economic problem, an obstacle to growth, a tax on investments, and a tax on the poor. We suggest that when legislatures carry out their constitutionally mandated functions (overseeing the executive, scrutinizing public expenditures and holding the government to account) effectively, they contribute in a significant way to reduced corruption.

In Chapter 3, we consider whether, how, and to what extent legislatures can help reduce corruption. While we focus primarily on the oversight function, we also consider the legislative/policy making and representation functions and how legislatures can play a meaningful role in multi-stakeholder networks and coalitions to control corruption. In Chapter 4, we present a comparative case study of how legislatures in two countries—Ghana and Nigeria—have helped combat corruption. We also show that there is a link between the effectiveness of a legislature's oversight, and hence ability to curb corruption, and social trust in parliament. In Chapter 5, we explore the relationship between social trust and political will further—and present a dynamic model on how public confidence in politicians impacts the latter's political will to take action.

In the next two chapters, we examine the other side of the coin: how legislatures can free themselves from corruption, gain citizen trust, and develop the (political) will to oversee and fight corruption. In Chapter 6, we look at a particular type of corruption—legislative corruption—and review some of the mechanisms, such as the codes of ethics and codes of conduct and the introduction of electoral recall which have been adopted to help reduce such corruption. We consider the differences between codes of ethics and codes of conduct, and review some of the problems in developing codes. In Chapter 7, we analyze electoral laws, campaign financing, and party political financing, all the time considering how legislatures can reduce corruption in these areas.

In Chapter 8, we summarize our main findings and present some practical advice on how to improve legislative involvement in controlling corruption.

And finally, in an Expert Monograph commissioned by (Global Organization of Parliamentarians Against Corruption) (GOPAC), Roy Cullen presents guidance on how to prevent the laundering of corrupt money.

CORRUPTION

Types of Corruption

Jain (2001) identifies three types of corruption: grand corruption, bureaucratic corruption, and legislative corruption. These three types of corruption ". . . differ from each other in terms of the types of decisions that are influenced by corruption, by the source of (misused) power by the decision-maker" (p. 73).

Grand corruption, as its name implies, is large and usually involves political leaders, the latter being defined by Jain (2001, p. 105) as those ". . . that

[have] worked out an equilibrium relationship [with their] constituents and [are] able to make and implement economic and political decisions." As elected officials, government leaders are expected to make economic and financial decisions that further the interests of their principals—the citizens who elected them. Jain points out that they have to balance the interests of the electorate at large with their own desire to stay in power. Corrupt leaders can change national policies to serve their own interests, at some cost to citizens.

Bureaucratic corruption, also known as petty corruption, refers to distortions in implementing such laws, policies, and regulations. In its most common form, civil servants demand small bribes from the public to receive a service to which they are entitled, receive a service to which they are not entitled, or simply to speed up a bureaucratic procedure.

Finally, legislative corruption refers to ". . . the manner and the extent to which the voting behavior of legislators can be influenced. Legislators can be bribed by interest groups to enact legislation that [favors their clients/members]. This type of conduct . . . include[s] vote-buying, whether by legislators in their attempts to get re-elected or by officials in the executive branch in their efforts to have some legislation enacted" (Jain, 2001, p. 75).

While opening up interesting questions for research, scholars and practitioners alike have found it difficult to operationalize these types of corruption and have tended to use proxies—most notable of which is Transparency International's Corruptions Perceptions Index—for more generalized corruption.

Costs of Corruption

Research has affirmed significant negative impact of corruption on economic growth. Mauro's (1997) examination of more than 100 countries offered a quantitative estimate of this effect. He found that if a given country was to improve its corruption score by 2.38 points on a 10-point scale, its annual per capita GDP growth would rise by over half a percentage point (Mauro, 1997, p. 91). Drury, Krieckhaus, and Lusztig (2006) demonstrate that corruption has a significant negative effect on countries that are not democratic (but interestingly, no significant effect on growth in democracies).

Causes of Corruption

Thomas and Meagher (2004) note that causal analysis of corruption typically falls into one of two broad approaches. The first focuses on structural or contextual causes, such as the structure and history of the political regime, culture, values, norms, and loyalties. A rich literature exists regarding the patrimonial state (e.g., Weber, 1964; Scott, 1972), social relationships (e.g., Cartier-Bresson, 1997; Fitchett and Ignatius, 2002; Yao, 2002), and unchecked government (e.g., Scott, 1972; Johnston, 1999; Moore et al., 1999). Here, the studies often draw upon institutional theory.

The second approach emphasizes the incentives that drive individuals to choose unethical acts. Klitgaard's (1988) formula explaining corruption (Corruption = Monopoly + Discretion – Accountability) provides a framework for further analysis. Corruption will exist when an official has monopoly power, with unfettered discretion and a lack of accountability. Scholars have looked at these, and related, factors that encourage corruption. For example, Rose-Ackerman (1998) and Shleifer and Vishny (1993) examined opportunity (discretionary authority), while Besley and McLaren (1993) considered the impact of low wages on corruption and Tyler (1990) and Polinsky and Shavell (2001) analyzed sanctions that discourage corrupt behavior. Underlying much of this work is the principal–agent model. For instance, Becker and Stigler (1974), Banfield (1975), Rose-Ackerman (1975, 1978), and Klitgaard (1988, 1991) treat the government official's hierarchical superior as the principal who has the problem of preventing the agent from engaging in fraudulent acts. Alternatively, the principal can be the legislature (acting on behalf of citizens) or citizens themselves.

Both approaches make reference to the importance of legislatures, but there have been few attempts to study the relationship between legislatures and corruption, and there is no consensus on the results. Under the first approach, scholars such as Treisman (2000) and Persson et al. (1997) have looked at the relationship between form of government and corruption and found that countries with more clearly demarcated political powers (i.e., those with presidential forms of government) have lower levels of corruption. By contrast, Gerring and Thacker (2004), Gerring, Thacker, and Moreno (2005), and Lederman et al. (2005) discovered that nations with fewer veto points in the political system (i.e., those where executive and legislative functions are fused, as in parliamentary systems) have lower levels of corruption. There are fewer studies under the second approach, but noteworthy are Pelizzo and Stapenhurst (2008) and Stapenhurst (2011), which found that countries with more oversight tools (i.e., where legislatures, acting as principals, have more tools with which to oversee actions by the executive) have lower levels of wrongdoing.

This paucity of research is surprising, as there appears to be agreement that multifaceted strategies are required to address corruption, and that one of the key components of such strategies is legislative oversight (Kaufmann and Dininio, 2006; Johnston and Kpundeh, 2001). Controlling corruption through case-by-case investigation and enforcement is not enough. Effort also needs to be made to reduce corruption opportunities, improve political accountability and increase civil society participation, increase economic competition, and enhance incentives for good performance. Such reforms target the relationships among core state institutions, the interactions between the state and firms, and the relationship between the state and civil society, the political system, and public administration. Figure 1.1, which presents a strategic framework proposed by the World Bank, is illustrative.[1]

However, this—and other—frameworks failed to note fully the importance of legislatures. In this case, the model ignores the linkages between

| **Institutional restraints on power**
• Independent and effective judiciary
• Independent prosecution,
  enforcement
• *Legislative oversight**
• *Supreme audit institution* | **Political accountability**
• Political competition
• Transparency in party financing
• Asset declarations,
  conflict of interest rules
• *Freedom of information*
• Investigative journalism |

Civil society participation
• *Public hearings of draft laws*
• Citizen oversight
• Role for NGOs

Anti-corruption

Competitive private sector
• Economic policy reform
• Competitive restructuring of monopolies
• Regulatory quality/simplification
• Transparency in corporate governance
• Collective business associations

Public sector management
• Meritocratic civil service with adequate pay
• Budget management (coverage, treasury, procurement, audit)
• Tax and customs
• Sectoral service delivery (health, education, energy)
• Decentralization with accountability

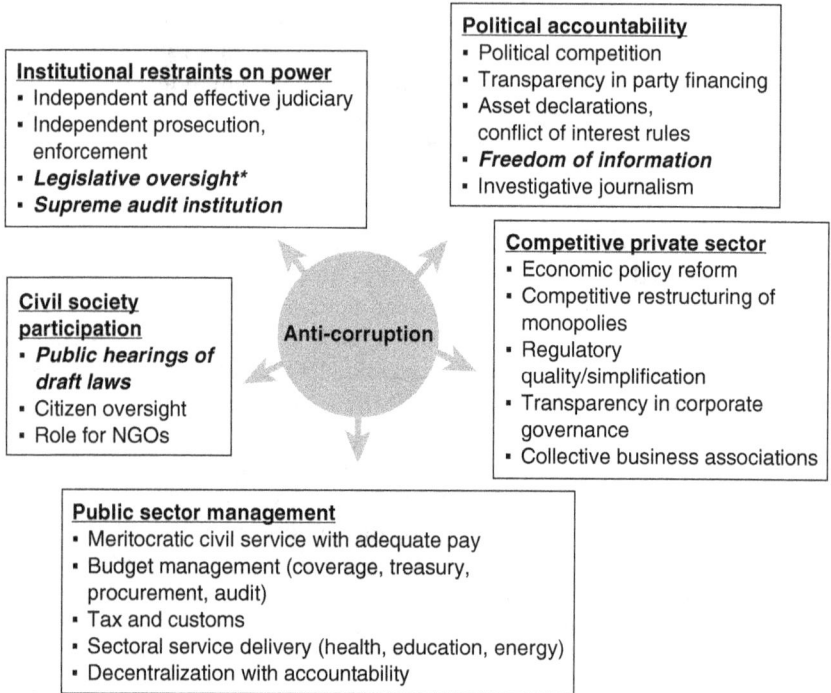

Figure 1.1   A Multifaceted Anti-corruption Strategy

* Mechanisms in italics refer to legislative oversight tools.
Source: Adapted from Kaufmann and Dininio (2006)

supreme audit institutions and the legislature (institutional restraints on power), the role of legislative committees in holding public hearings on draft laws (civil society participation), and political competition and campaign finance rules (political accountability). Also missing is the role of the legislature in developing ethics regimes and codes of conduct for members of the executive, legislature, and bureaucracy.

In short, our knowledge of corruption is wide-ranging and comprehensive, but there are significant gaps. There is general agreement on the definition and costs of corruption and on some of the strategies to combat it. The role of the legislature and of individual legislators is acknowledged but not well developed. Similarly, national anti-corruption strategy frameworks highlight the importance of legislative oversight, supreme audit institutions, public hearings of draft laws, and freedom of information but fail to "knit" these, and other, elements of legislative oversight together. But if the literature regarding the role of the legislature in controlling corruption is lacking, the literature on legislatures equally lacks a focus on the desired outcomes of oversight, one of which is reduced corruption.

LEGISLATURES

Legislative Oversight

There is no consensus on the definition of legislative oversight (Olson, 2008) and, like the broader field of legislative studies, the concept is under-theorized. There are few global analyses, the principles of which are Gerring and Thacker (2004), Lederman et al., (2005), Doig and Theobald (2000), Hope (2000), Persson et al. (1997), and Treisman (2000). Most research is undertaken at a country or regional level, often within a loose theoretical framework (e.g., Olson and Norton, 1996; Norton and Ahmed, 1999). These investigations typically examine legislative functions within countries more generally, and do not focus solely, or particularly, on oversight. Furthermore, while there is a plethora of studies on the oversight function in the United States, there are only a small number of studies outside it.

Scholars have proposed different definitions for oversight. Schick (1976) noted that it consists of legislative supervision of the policies and programs enacted by government. Others, such as Ogul (1976) and Maffio (2002), suggested that it is not just supervision of what the executive branch of government has done, but also supervision of the executive's legislative proposals. By contrast, Olson and Mezey (1991) and McCubbins and Schwartz (1984) argued that oversight refers to the set of activities that a parliament performs to evaluate the implementation of policies.[2] Some academicians, such as Doering (1995), Drewry (1989), Blondel (1973), and Olson (2008), distinguished between oversight and scrutiny.

In a Research Paper of the National Democratic Institute (2000, p. 19), legislative oversight was defined as "the obvious follow-on activity linked to lawmaking. After participating in law-making, the legislature's main role is to see whether laws are effectively implemented and whether, in fact, they address and correct the problems as intended by their drafters." This definition captures the role that parliaments play in overseeing government policies and activities after they have been enacted, but it overlooks that parliaments may be engaged in oversight activities well before a policy is enacted. Parliaments oversee the executive not only with regard to the execution and implementation of policies but also with regard to the preparation of policies. This is why paraphrasing Lees's (1977) definition of legislative oversight,[3] this book refers to legislative oversight of the executive as "the behavior of legislators and their staff which affects executive behavior."

Researchers have also paid attention to the tools that parliaments and legislatures can employ to government activities. Studies have underlined that the legislatures may adopt several tools such as hearings in committees, hearings in the plenary assembly, the creation of inquiry committees, parliamentary questions, question time, the interpellations, and the ombudsperson (Maffio, 2002; Pennings, 2000). Others have noted, however, that the presence of oversight tools is a necessary but insufficient condition for effective oversight. Effective oversight, as was observed, depends not only on the availability of tools, but also on additional conditions such as oversight powers given to the parliament, whether the parliament has the ability to modify legislation (Loewenberg and Patterson, 1979), whether parliaments and parliamentarians are given proper information to perform their oversight tasks adequately (Frantzich, 1979), the role of individual MPs, the role of committee chairs, the saliency of issues, and how aggressively the opposition performs its role (Rockman, 1984).

In overseeing the executive, parliaments have several different methods at their disposal. Damgaard (2000, p. 8) notes for example that the list of tools includes "ombudsmen, committees of inquiry, auditing institutions, specialized parliamentary committees, public hearings [and] interpellations that may end with a vote in the chamber." Other mechanisms include hearing in plenary sessions of the parliament, questions, question time, auditors general, and the public account committees (National Democratic Institute, 2000).

Some scholars have underlined that not all such tools are alike. Maffio (2002) and Maor (1999) have offered two alternative groupings. For Maffio (2002), they can be grouped on the basis of whether they are applied before or after a specific policy is implemented (hence she refers to *ex ante* and *ex post* oversight), and she further argued that some have more bite than others. Maor (1999) argued instead that tools take either the form of specific bodies (ombudsman, committees, and so on) or the form of a procedure (interpellation, questions, and so on). Alternatively, one could consider whether the oversight methods are established inside (questions, question time, interpellations, hearings, and public account committees) or outside (ombudsmen and auditors general) the parliament.

Some studies have investigated the relationship between oversight tools and various political as well as socio-economic conditions (Maffio, 2002; Pelizzo and Stapenhurst, 2004; Pennings, 2000). The most important conclusion is that oversight is not solely the derivative of other variables but has a dynamic of its own. Pennings (2000) found that patterns of oversight could not be reduced to what Castles (1998) calls "families of nations,"[4] to the distinction between consensus and majoritarian democracies (Lijphart, 1999) and not even, contra Linz (1994), to the distinction between presidential and parliamentary system. While Pelizzo and Stapenhurst (2004) showed that parliamentary systems are on average better equipped to perform this function, later work has shown that the form of government has no statistical influence on the effectiveness of oversight and its ability to influence the functioning of a political system. Pelizzo and Stapenhurst (2006) showed in this respect that while the number of oversight devices and the level of socio-economic development are key determinants of whether a country is formally democratic and liberal democratic, the probability that it is formally or liberal democratic is not significantly related to the form of government once controlled for the number of oversight tools and level of development.

In short, the literature on legislative oversight is confused, with no consensus even on the definition of oversight, and largely descriptive regarding oversight tools and how they are exercised. A small but growing body of empirical work supports the importance of oversight, but again results are conflicting.

Legislation/Policy-Making

A decade ago, Wilton Park (2003) reported that there has been a general lack of political will to implement the necessary legislation to combat corruption. Indeed, failure to enact legislation was said to be one of the biggest obstacles to curbing corruption. Mobilizing parliamentarians to take corruption seriously, and to enact constitutional and legislative amendments, was said to be one of the first steps in establishing an efficient anti-corruption regime. At the same time, however, simply enacting a plethora of laws alone is insufficient; the implementation of laws must be overseen, and those responsible for their implementation must be given the necessary resources to make the laws work.

Legislation needs to be anticipatory rather than reactive. It has been argued (Wilton Park, 2003) that policy-makers need to follow actively and anticipate new practices and trends in corruption and to take more seriously the results of expert research. Standardization and harmonization of police and prosecution and judicial statistics can improve information about trends in corruption. Preventive legislation could harmonize the actions of different agencies and could increase their efficiency. Legislators need to ensure that anti-corruption legislation is in fact primarily aimed to reduce corruption and is not merely window-dressing. Nevertheless, shortcomings in legislation should not be an excuse for not implementing the law in one specific area or another.

Representation

Figure 1.1 shows that civil society and non-governmental organizations (NGOs) play an important role in curbing corruption. Here, the representative function of legislatures can provide synergy and reinforcement. Parliament can organize public hearings, thereby providing a forum for civil society groups and individual citizens to have their voices heard. NGOs can also lobby parliament and parliamentarians to take the issue of corruption more seriously—thereby helping boost political will to tackle the problem. In turn, members of parliament can raise issues of concern with ministers and other officials, and direct citizen complaints about corruption to the appropriate agencies, such as the ombuds office, the police, or the anti-corruption commission.

CONCLUSION

Corruption is a multi-faceted problem, one that is increasingly referenced in the public media and targeted through public and private "anti-corruption campaigns." It is generally recognized that parliaments have a key role to play in helping curb corruption, and that they can do this through their core functions of oversight, legislation, and representation. At the same time, however, parliaments are perceived by the public to be part of the problem of corruption—with legislative corruption being a heretofore understudied type of corruption.

In this book, we look at the problem of corruption, its costs and consequences, and the role that parliament can play in reducing corruption. We also look at legislative corruption, examining in detail unethical behavior of legislators and problems of political financing and electoral fraud. Throughout, our analyses are grounded in up-to-date empirical analyses, yet our conclusions and recommendations are simple and practical.

NOTES

1. Transparency International proposes a similar multifaceted strategy, using the notion of "pillars of integrity," where one such pillar is legislative oversight.
2. However, Rockman (1984) and Ogul and Rockman (1990) noted that there is much greater variety as to how oversight can be defined, and that definitions of oversight range from minimalistic to all-encompassing.
3. Lees defined oversight as "the behavior by legislators and their staffs, individually or collectively, which results in an impact, intended or not, on bureaucratic behavior."
4. The logic of the "families of nations" approach was outlined by Castles (1998); it considers that social and policy outcomes within a country are derived from "affinities of decent, imperial ties, common legal or religious cultures, diffusion and membership of political and economic unions."

REFERENCES

Banfield, E. (1975). Corruption as a Feature of Governmental Organization. *Journal of Law and Economics*, 18(3), 587–605.

Becker, G., and G. Stigler. (1974). Law Enforcement, Malfeasance and Compensation of Enforcers. *Journal of Legal Studies*, 13(1), 1–19.

Besley, T., and J. McLaren. (1993). Taxes and Bribery: The Role of Wage Incentives. *The Economic Journal*, 103, 119–141.

Blondel, J. (1973). *Comparative Legislatures*. Englewood Cliffs, NJ: Prentice Hall.

Cartier-Bresson, J. (1997). Corruption Networks, Transaction Security and Illegal Social Exchange. *Political Studies*, 45(3), 463–476.

Castles, F. G. (1998). *Comparative Public Policy: Patterns of Post-war Transformation*. Cheltenham, UK: Edward Elgar.

Damgaard, E. (2000). Representation, Delegation and Parliamentary Control. Paper prepared for the workshop on "Parliamentary Control of the Executive," ECPR Joint Sessions of Workshops, Copenhagen, April 14–19.

Doering, H. (Ed.). (1995). *Parliaments and Majority Rule in Western Europe.* New York, NY: St. Martin's Press.
Doig, A., and R. Theobald. (2000). *Corruption and Democratisation.* London: Frank Cass.
Drewry, G. (Ed.) (1989). *The New Select Committees.* Oxford, UK: Clarendon Press.
Drury, Cooper, Jonathan Krieckhaus, and Michael Lusztig. (2006). Corruption, Democracy and Economic Growth. *International Political Science Review* 27(2), 121–136.
Fitchett, J., and D. Ignatius. (2002, February 1). Lengthy ELF Inquiry Nears Explosive Finish *International Herald Tribune*
Frantzich, S. (1979). "Who Makes Our Laws? The Legislative Effectiveness of Members of the U.S. Congress." Legislative Studies Quarterly 4(3): 409–428.
Gerring, J., and S. Thacker. (2004). Political Institutions and Corruption: The Role of Unitism and Parliamentarism. *British Journal of Political Science,* 34, 295–330.
Gerring, J., S. Thacker, and C. Moreno. (2005). A Centripetal Theory of Democratic Governance: A Global Inquiry. *American Political Science Review,* (Nov.) 567–581.
Hope, K.R. (2000) Corruption and Development in Africa. In K.R. Hope, Sr. and B.C. Chikulu (Eds.) *Corruption and Development in Africa. Lessons from Country Case-Studies,* pp. 17–39. New York: St. Martin's Press.
Huntington, S.P. (1968). *Political Order in Changing Societies.* New Haven, Connecticut: Yale University Press.
Jain, A.K. (2001). *Political Economy of Corruption.* London: Routledge.
Johnston, M. (1999). What Can Be Done About Entrenched Corruption? In S. Kpundeh and R. Stapenhurst (Eds.) *Curbing Corruption: Toward a Model for Building National Integrity,* pp. 13–18. Washington, DC: World Bank.
Johnston, M., and S. Kpundeh. (2001). Anticorruption Coalitions and Sustainable Reform. Unpublished Manuscript. Washington, DC: World Bank.
Kaufmann, Daniel. (2000). Governance and Anticorruption. In Vinod Thomas et al. (Eds.) *The Quality of Growth.* New York: Oxford University Press.
Kaufmann, D., and P. Dininio. (2006). Corruption: A Key Challenge for Development. In R. Stapenhurst, N. Johnston, and R. Pelizzo (Eds.) *The Role of Parliament in Curbing Corruption,* pp. 13–24. Washington, DC: World Bank.
Klitgaard, R. (1988). *Controlling Corruption* Berkeley, CA: University of California Press.
Klitgaard, R. (1991). Gifts and Bribes. In Zeckhauser, R (Ed.) *Strategy and Choice,* pp. 211–240. Cambridge, MA: MIT Press.
Kunicova, J., and S. Rose-Ackerman. (2005). Electoral Rules and Constitutional Structures as Constraints on Corruption. *British Journal of Political Science,* 35, 573–606.
Kunicova, J., and S. Rose-Ackerman. (2007). Electoral Rules and Constitutional Structures as Constraints on Corruption, *Conference Working Papers: Corruption and Accountability.* Vancouver, BC: University of British Columbia.
Lees, John D. (1977). Legislatures and Oversight: A Review Article on a Neglected Area of Research. *Legislative Studies Quarterly* 2(2), 193–208.
Lederman, D., N. Loayza, and R. Soares. (2001). Accountability and Corruption: Political Institutions do Matter, *Policy Research Working Paper 2708,* Washington, DC: The World Bank.
Lederman, D., N. Loayza, and R. Soares (2005). Accountability and Corruption: Political Institutions Do Matter. *Economics and Politics,* 17 (March), 1–35.
Lijphart, A. (1999). *Patterns of Democracy.* New Haven, Yale University Press.
Linz, J.J. (1994). Presidential or Parliamentary: Does it Make a Difference? In J.J. Linz and A. Valenzuela (Eds.), *The Failure of Presidential Democracy,* pp. 3–91. Baltimore, Johns Hopkins University Press.

Loewenberg, G., and S.C. Patterson (1979) Comparing Legislatures. Boston: Little, Brown.

Maffio, R. (2002). Quis custodiet ipsos custodes? Il controllo parlamentare dell'attivita' di governo in prospettiva comparata. *Quaderni di Scienza Politica*, 9(2), 333–383.

Maor, M. (1999). Electoral Competition and the Oversight Game: A Transaction Cost Approach and the Norwegian Experience. *European Journal of Political Research*, 35, 371–388.

Mauro, P. (1997). The Effects of Corruption on Growth, Investment and Government Expenditure: A Cross Country Analysis. In K.A. Elliot (Ed.) *Corruption and the Global Economy*, pp. 371–388. Washington D.C.: Institute for International Economics.

McCubbins, M., and T. Schwartz. (1984). Congressional Oversight Overlooked: Police Patrols versus Fire Alarms. *American Journal of Political Science*, 28(1), 165–179.

Moore, M., J. Leavy, P. Houtzager, and H. White. (1999). *Polity Qualities: How Governance Affects Poverty.* Unpublished mimeo.

Naím, M. (1994). Latin America: The Second Stage of Reform. *Journal of Democracy*, 5(4), 32–48.

National Democratic Institute for International Affairs. (2000). Strengthening Legislative Capacity in Legislative-Executive Relations. *Legislative Research Series*, paper no. 6, Washington D.C.

Neff, N.H. (1964). Economic Development through Bureaucratic Corruption. *The American Behavioral Scientist*, November, 8(2), 8–14.

Norton, P., and N. Ahmed. (1999). Legislatures in Asia: Exploring Diversity. In P. Norton and N. Ahmed (Eds.) *Legislatures in Developmental Perspective*, pp. 1–12. London: Frank Cass.

Ogul, M.S. (1976). *Congress Oversees the Bureaucracy: Studies in Legislative Supervision.* Pittsburg, PA: University of Pittsburgh Press.

Ogul, M., and B. Rockman. (1990). Overseeing Oversight: New Departures and old Problems. *Legislative Studies Quarterly*, 15(1), 5–24.

Olson, D. (2008). Legislatures and Administration in Oversight and Budgets: Constraints, Means and Executives. In R. Stapenhurst, R. Pelizzo, D. Olson, and L. von Trapp (Eds.) *Legislative Oversight and Budgeting: A World Perspective*, pp. 323–331. Washington, D.C.: World Bank.

Olson, D., and P. Norton (Eds.). (1996). *The New Parliaments of Central and Eastern Europe.* London: Frank Cass.

Olson, D.M., and M.L. Mezey (Eds.). (1991). *Legislatures in the Policy Process: The Dilemmas of Economic Policy.* Cambridge: Cambridge University Press.

Pelizzo, R., and R. Stapenhurst. (2004). Tools for Legislative Oversight Policy. *World Bank Research Working Paper.* Washington, D.C.: World Bank.

Pelizzo, R., and R. Stapenhurst. (2006). Democracy and Oversight. Paper presented at the 102nd Annual Meeting of the American Political Science Association, Philadelphia, PA. August 31–September 3.

Pelizzo, R., and R. Stapenhurst. (2008). Tools for Legislative Oversight: An Empirical Investigation. In R. Stapenhurst, R. Pelizzo, D. Olson, and L. von Trapp (Eds.) *Legislative Oversight and Budgeting: A World Perspective.* Washington D.C.: The World Bank Institute.

Pennings, Paul. (2000). Parliamentary Control of the Executive in 47 Democracies. Paper prepared for the workshop on Parliamentary Control of the Executive, ECPR Joint Sessions of Workshops, Copenhagen, April 14–19.

Persson, P., G. Roland, and G. Tabellini. (1997). Separation of Powers and Political Accountability. *Quarterly Journal of Economics Perspectives*, 112, 1163–1202.

Polinsky, A., and S. Shavell. (2001). Corruption and Optimal Law Enforcement. *Journal of Public Economics,* 81(1), 1–24.

Rockman, B. A. (1984). Legislative—Executive Relations and Legislative Oversight. *Legislative Studies Quarterly,* 9(3), 387–440.

Rose-Ackerman, S. (1975). The Economics of Corruption. *Journal of Public Economics,* 13(2), 182–203.

Rose-Ackerman, S. (1978). *Corruption. A Study in Political Economy.* London/New York: Academic Press.

Rose-Ackerman, S. (1998). Corruption and the Global Economy in the United Nations Development Program. *Corruption and Integrity Improvement Initiatives in Developing Countries.* New York: United Nations.

Schick, A. (1976). Congress and the Details of Administration. *Public Administration Review,* 36, 516–528.

Scott, J.C. (1972). *Comparative Political Corruption.* Englewood Cliffs, NJ: Prentice Hall.

Shleifer, A., and R. Vishny. (1993). Corruption. *The Quarterly Journal of Economics,* 108(3), 599–617.

Stapenhurst, Frederick (Rick). (2011). *Legislative Oversight and Curbing Corruption; Presidentialism and Parliamentarianism Revisited.* Unpublished PhD thesis. Canberra: Australian National University.

Thomas, M., and P. Meagher. (2004). A Corruption Primer: An Overview of Concepts in the Corruption Literature. *The IRIS Discussion Papers on Institutions and Development,* 04/03 College Park, MD: University of Maryland.

Treisman, Daniel (2000). The Causes of Corruption: A Cross National Study. *Journal of Public Economics,* 399–457.

Tyler, T. (1990). *Why People Obey the Law.* New Haven, CT: Yale University Press.

Weber, M. (1964). *The Theory of Social and Economic Organization.* New York, NY: Free Press.

Wei, S-J., and D. Kaufmann. (1998). Does "Grease Money" Speed Up the Wheels of Commerce? *International Monetary Fund* (Washington, D.C.). Available at: www.imf.org/external/pubs/cat/longres.cfm?sk=3524.0

Wilton Park. (2003). *The Role of Government and Parliament in Curbing Corruption in Central and Eastern Europe.* Conference 704. March 3–6, 2003.

Yao, S. (2002). Privilege and Corruption: The Problems of China's Socialist Market Economy. *American Journal of Economics and Sociology,* 61(1), 279–299.

2 The Dividends of Good Governance

INTRODUCTION

As we noted in Chapter 1, for many years, scholars and practitioners alike did not pay sufficient attention to corruption. However, empirical research carried out from the mid-1990s onward has made clear not only that corruption is detrimental for the quality of democracy, that it is a political problem, and that it has a devastating impact on economic growth and development, but also that the reduction of corruption may provide a major stimulus to economic growth, and that anti-corruption activities are an essential component of any successful development strategy.

The purpose of the present chapter is to show, on empirical grounds, how detrimental corruption is for socio-economic development. In the course of this chapter, we will show that while there are several ways in which development can be measured, corruption is harmful to development regardless of how it is measured.

This chapter is organized in the following way. In the first section, we discuss the conditions under which corruption is believed to flourish. In so doing, we will point out that there are three set of factors that seem to play a particularly significant role in facilitating corruption: poverty, lack of institutionalization, and the nature of the economy. Specifically we will argue that in countries plagued by extreme poverty, where political institutions are inadequately developed, where the state is not adequately insulated from social pressures, and where the economy is not sufficiently competitive, corruption is expected to thrive.

In the second section, we will show that corruption is detrimental for development. After discussing what is development and how it can be measured, we show that countries with higher levels of corruption are poorer, have lower rates of literacy, higher rates of infant mortality, shorter life expectancy, fewer motor vehicles per capita, and a more backward, agriculture-based economy, whereas the opposite is true in countries with less corruption.

Building on the simple statistical analyses presented in the second section, in the third section we present the results of more sophisticated statistical analyses. By doing so we are able to show how much a country can improve in terms of education, wealth, industrialization, motorization, and quality of life thanks to little improvements in the level of good governance and transparency. In the fourth and final section, we draw some conclusions.

CORRUPTION: CAUSES AND CONSEQUENCES

In Chapter 1 we identified several conditions that facilitate the emergence of corruption and corrupt practices. In this section, we will focus on three conditions that we believe are of particular importance: poverty, the degree of political institutionalization, and the nature of the economy.

Research has shown that in countries that are confronted with extreme poverty, the population does not have the time or the inclination to be concerned with the state of the democracy (e.g., Huntington, 1991) and the level of corruption. In extremely poor countries, citizens have greater incentives to tolerate corruption and bribes: Bribes represent a way to gain access to resources that are scarce and otherwise unobtainable, such as health care. Alternatively, they are used as a means to increase an income that otherwise would not enable the corrupt individuals to sustain themselves. Moreover, poverty favors corruption because in very poor countries, there are fairly low rates of literacy and, therefore, the population does not have the means to be properly informed and to play an active role in monitoring and curbing corruption.

The lack of institutionalization is strongly connected with corruption. There are many studies, from Huntington (1968) to Evans (1989, 1995), that have underlined how the inadequate institutionalization—that is, an inadequate political development prevents the state, its organs, and its bureaucracy—from enjoying a certain level of autonomy from society and social pressures. In a poorly institutionalized context, the state and its organs are not able and are not equipped, to resist social pressures and requests, and this inability is believed to facilitate the proliferation of nepotism, clientelism, and corruption. Not surprisingly, Evans (1989, 1995) pointed out, that it is precisely where the state is poorly institutionalized, that the state is inadequately insulated from social pressure, and becomes what Evans calls a "predatory state." In addition, the absence of adequate mechanisms of inter-institutional control, such as the tools for parliamentary oversight, together with the unpredictability of the judiciary, may contribute to corruption (Pelizzo and Stapenhurst, 2012).

The nature of the economy plays a key role in favoring corruption. Research studies have underlined the importance of two aspects in this regard: the role of the state in the economy, and the nature of economic competition in a country. With regard to the former, the World Development Report (1997) showed that where the state creates an artificial gap between the supply of, and demand for, public services, or where it tolerates wide margins of bureaucratic discretion, it creates the condition for corruption. If there is too much state intervention in the economy, an excessive supply of state services, too many regulations for business, too many taxes or if the taxation rate is too high, and/or if rules are arbitrarily implemented, the state, perhaps inadvertently, facilitates the proliferation of corrupt practices.

Similarly, if the economy is not adequately competitive, corruption arises. In those countries in which the market is not competitive, either because the market is a monopoly or an oligopoly, there are a small number of economic actors who can solve their collective action problems, reach agreements, get organized, and put pressure on the government and the state in order to obtain (private) benefits and gains.

While poverty, inadequate institutionalization, and the nature of the economy may be regarded as the causes of corruption, the literature has also paid considerable attention to the fact that corruption may have far reaching consequences. We already noted, in Chapter 1, the significant negative impact of corruption on economic growth (Mauro, 1997).

Corruption can weaken economic growth through many channels. Unsound policies, unpredictable processes, and distorted public expenditures resulting from vested interests lead to macroeconomic instability, weakened property rights, reduced competition, inefficient allocation of resources, poor and deteriorated physical infrastructure, and smaller expenditures on education (Hellman, Jones, Kaufman and Zoido-Lobatón 2000; Tanzi and Davoodi, 1997; Mauro, 1997).

For businesses, corruption increases risks and uncertainty, entails payments that represent a kind of tax, and requires more management time spent negotiating with public officials. As a result, it dampens investment (Mauro, 1997; Wei and Kaufmann, 1998) and pushes firms into the unofficial economy (Friedman et al. 2000; Johnson, Kaufmann, McMillan, and Woodruff, 2000). Where corruption provides more lucrative opportunities than productive work, the allocation of talent also deteriorates (Murphy, Shleifer, and Vishny, 1991).

By misallocating resources, increasing transaction costs, and placing a "tax" on investments, corruption provides international investors with an incentive to invest their capital elsewhere. This contributes to a slowdown in economic growth and prevents countries from experiencing balanced development. The purpose of the next section is to present some evidence of the costs of corruption.

SOME EMPIRICAL EVIDENCE

While individuals engaged in, or benefiting from, corrupt activities may not be able to appreciate it, it is clear: The cost of corruption is massive and, as a result, corruption represents one of the major obstacles for socio-economic development.

With regard to development, scholars have generally agreed on the fact that development is an evolutionary process through which traditional forms of social organization (the clan, tribe, or group) are replaced by modern forms of social organization such as the state.[1] Most social theorists believe that social development, political development, and economic development are interconnected, and that social structure, culture, economy, and politics must all undergo some transformation as development occurs and that a society that fails to develop on each of these aspects cannot properly be regarded as developed.[2]

While researchers acknowledge that the process of development is a multifaceted one, it is generally agreed that economic development represents the core of the developmental process—a process that can be stimulated by social capital, appropriate institutional design, and appropriate policy intervention and that it can be hindered by the predatory behavior of the state, misallocation of resources, and by corruption (Kaufmann, 2000).[3]

With regard to the measurement of development, researchers have devised and employed several indicators of socio-economic development (Lipset, 1959). The reason why various indicators were adopted is that scholars generally acknowledged that development is a complex, multifaceted phenomenon, and that in order to capture each and every aspect of development, it was necessary to have very specific metrics.

In the course of the present analysis, we rely on six indicators of development: the literacy rate, the percentage of the employed population working in the agricultural sector, the country's wealth as indicated by the Gross National Income(GNI) per capita, the life expectancy at birth, the infant mortality rate, and the number of motor vehicles in the country. Literacy rate provides an indication of a country's level of education, the percentage of people working in the agricultural sector provides an indication of the industrialization of the country, the country's wealth is the preeminent indicator of development, the infant mortality and the life expectancy variables provide an indication of the state capacity and quality of the health care system, while the number of motor vehicles reflects not just the level of motorization of transports but also the level of wealth—for people have more cars in richer countries than in poorer ones.

We collected information on each of these six variables from the World Bank development dataset. Data were collected for the following countries: Algeria, Andorra, Antigua and Barbuda, Argentina, Armenia, Austria, Bahrain, Bangladesh, Benin, Bhutan, Bulgaria, Burkina Faso, Burundi, Cambodia, Cameroon, Canada, Central African Republic, Chile, Congo (Democratic Republic), Costa Rica, Cote d'Ivoire, Croatia, Cyprus, Czech Republic, Djibouti, Estonia, Finland, France, Gabon, Georgia, Germany, Ghana, Greece, Grenada, Haiti, Hungary, Iceland, Indonesia, Ireland, Iran,

Israel, Jamaica, Japan, Jordan, Kenya, Korea (Democratic Republic), Latvia, Lebanon, Lesotho, Liberia, Liechtenstein, Lithuania, Luxembourg, Malaysia, Marshall Islands, Mauritius, Moldova, Monaco, Morocco, Namibia, Netherlands, New Zealand, Nicaragua, Norway, Palau, Paraguay, Philippines, Poland, Qatar, San Marino, Senegal, Serbia, Seychelles, Singapore, Slovak Republic, Slovenia, Spain, Sri Lanka, Switzerland, Tajikistan, Tanzania, Thailand, Togo, Tonga, Trinidad and Tobago, Tunisia, Turkey, Uganda, Ukraine, United Kingdom, Uruguay, Vietnam, Yemen, and Zimbabwe.

A simple statistical analysis provides an indication of values taken by each of the six variables in our 94-country sample. Details are presented in Table 2.1.

Table 2.1 reveals that while most of the minimum values (reported in the third column) are an indication of underdevelopment, in the case of infant mortality and employment in the agricultural sector, the low value recorded in this column provides an indication of development. This is because development is believed to be associated with a high level of literacy, industrialization (as indicated by a small percentage of workers employed in agriculture), wealth, life expectancy, motorization, and a low infant mortality rate.

The data also make it clear that there is considerable variation in each of the variables under consideration. The number of cars per thousand people, for example, varies from a minimum of 3 to a maximum of 908 per thousand, infant mortality from a minimum of 1.8 per thousand to

Table 2.1   Descriptive Statistics

	Number of countries[1]	Minimum value	Maximum value	Mean	Standard deviation
Literacy rate	45	41.6	99.8	85.7	17.3
Employment in agriculture	44	1.1	65.6	12.5	15.6
GNI per capita	69	93	40,400	9,277	11,396
Life expectancy	88	46.7	83	70.6	9.9
Infant mortality	94	1.8	112.8	24.4	27.2
Motor vehicles per 1,000 people	56	3	908	346.5	241.0

[1] There is considerable variation in the amount of missing data across the various variables: while we have observations for 100 percent of the countries with regard to infant mortality (94 out of 94), the number of observations for the other variables is somewhat lower for life expectancy (88 out of 94, or 93.6 percent), 69 (or 73.4 percent) for GNI per capita, 56 (or 59.5 percent) for the number of motor vehicles, and it is respectively 44 and 45 (46.8 and 47.8 percent) for employment in agriculture and literacy rate.

112.8 per thousand, life expectancy from a minimum of about 47 years to a maximum of 83 years, wealth per capita from US $93 to US $40,400, employment in agriculture from a minimum of 1.1 percent of the total labor force to a maximum of nearly 66 percent, and the literacy rate varies from 41.6 percent to 99.8 percent. The standard deviation captures this very considerable variation.

We have computed an important descriptive statistic for the variables in our sample, namely the mean. The data presented in the fifth column show that in our sample the average literacy rate is 85.7 percent, that employment in agriculture averages 12.5 percent, that the GNI per capita is US $ is $9,277, that life expectancy is on average 70.6 years, that the average rate of infant mortality is 24.4 out of 1,000, and, finally, that there are on average 346.5 motor vehicles per thousand people.

The level of corruption for each of the countries included in our sample was measured on the basis of Transparency International's Corruption Perception Index (CPI). We use this measure of corruption for three reasons: 1) it is strongly, positively, and significantly related to other measures of corruption;[4] 2) since previous studies had already proved the relationship between corruption, as measured on the basis of World Bank's governance indicators and various measures of development, we wanted to test whether we would find a strong association/relationship between corruption (measured in a different way) and development; and 3) the number of countries for which Transparency International (TI) computed the CPI was much larger than the number of countries for which other measures of corruption, such as the one devised by Global Integrity, had been computed.

The CPI is a 10-point scale with a value of 10 when a country is totally free of corruption and a value of 0 when it has the maximum level of corruption. We have data for 86 of the 94 countries included in our sample. The CPI varies from a minimum of 1.8 to a maximum of 9.4, with an average value of 4.5. See Table 2.2 and Figure 2.1.

Once we correlate CPI with the six measures of development discussed above, we find that corruption is strongly and significantly related to each of the measures of development.[5] Details are presented in Table 2.3.

These correlation coefficients tell a fairly simple and straightforward story. They consistently indicate that countries that have less corruption

Table 2.2 Global Corruption (TI Corruption Perception Index [CPI])

	Number of observations	Minimum value	Maximum value	Mean	Standard deviation
CPI	86	1.8	9.4	4.515	2.2447

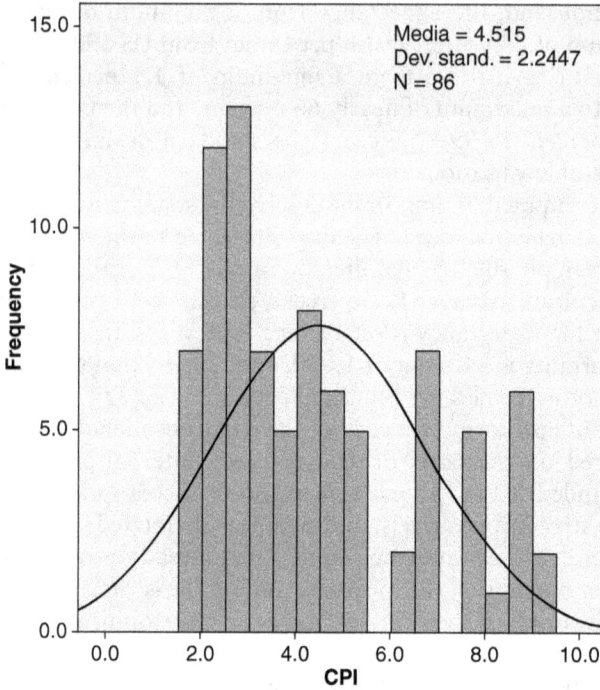

Figure 2.1   The Distribution of CPI (n = 86)

Table 2.3   Correlation Analysis (sig.)

	Literacy rate	Employment in agriculture	GNI per capita	Life expectancy	Infant mortality rate	Motor vehicles
CPI	.486	−.585	.866	.710	−.631	.734
	(.001)	(.000)	(.000)	(.000)	(.000)	(.000)

also have a higher literacy rate, are more industrialized, are richer, have a longer life expectancy, have lower infant mortality, and have more cars—in other words, benefit from the dividends of good governance. By contrast, countries with a higher level of corruption have fewer cars, higher infant mortality, shorter life, more poverty, less industrialization, and lower literacy. These are the costs of corruption.

The scatterplots presented in Figures 2.2 to 2.7 show graphically that development, however measured, is affected by good governance and corruption.

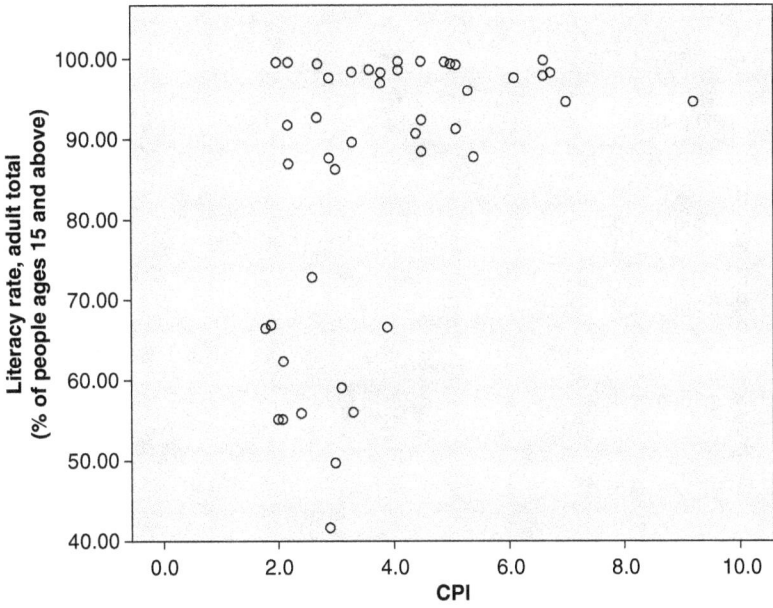

Figure 2.2   Corruption and Literacy Rate

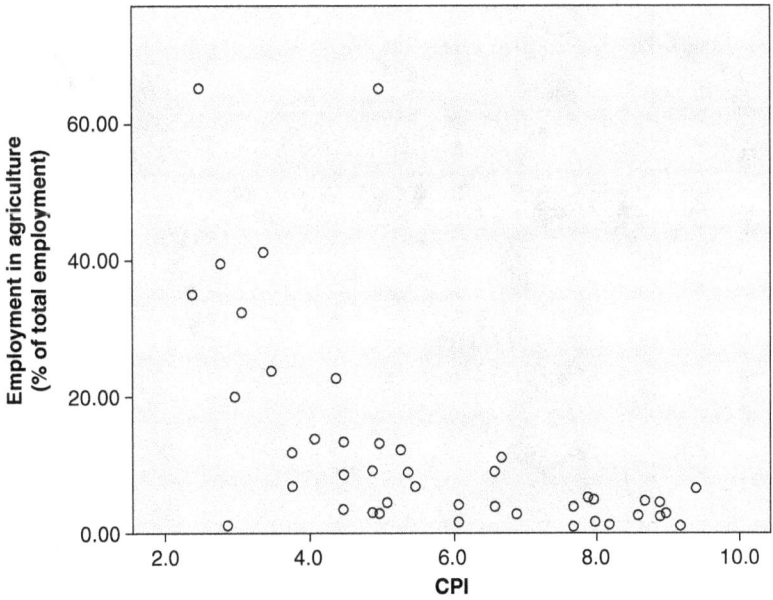

Figure 2.3   Corruption and Employment in Agriculture

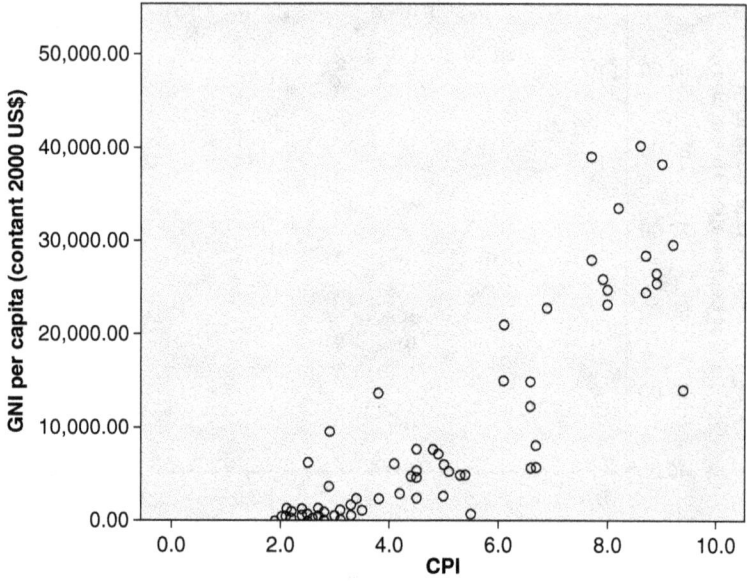

Figure 2.4 Corruption and GNI per Capita

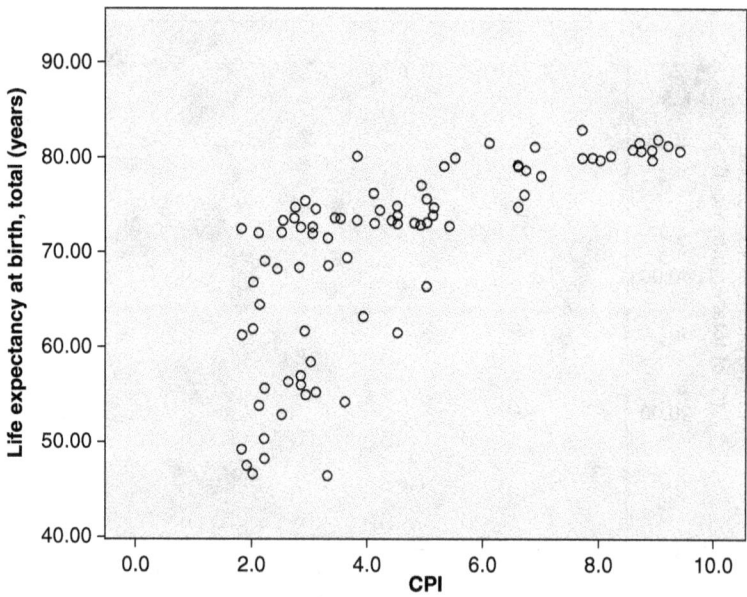

Figure 2.5 Corruption and Life Expectancy

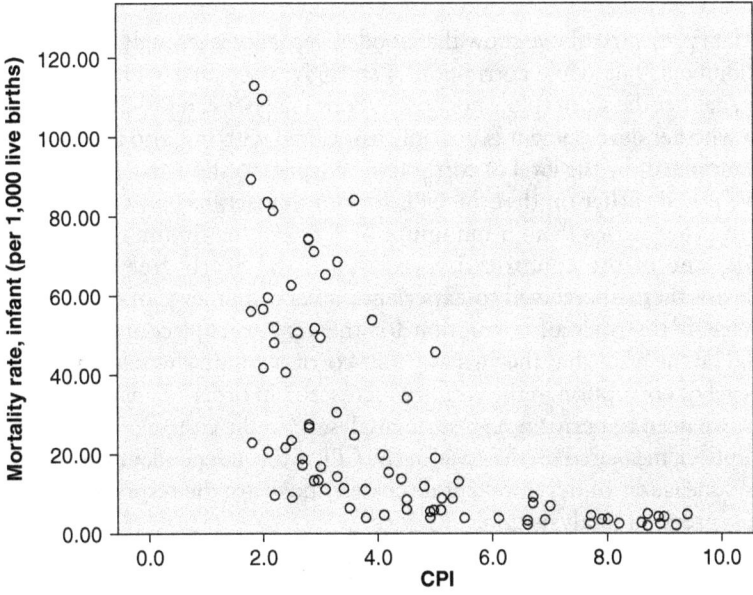

Figure 2.6   Corruption and Infant Mortality

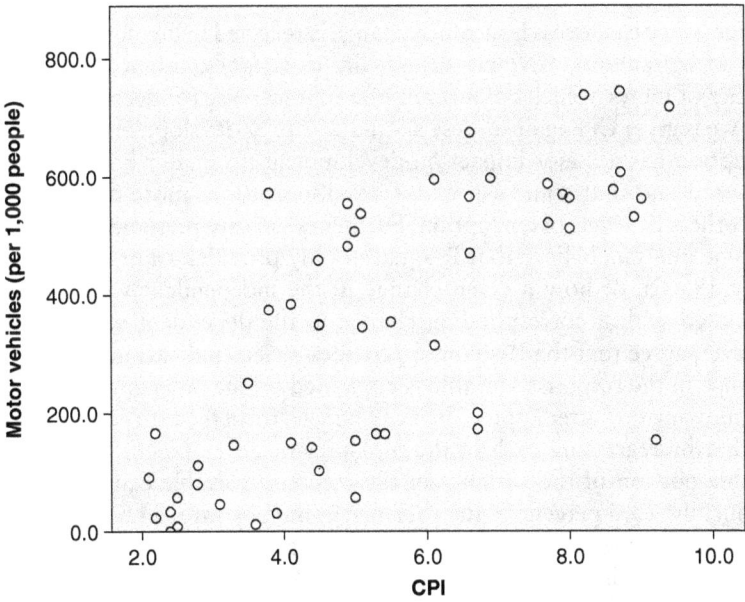

Figure 2.7   Number of Motor Vehicles

FROM ASSOCIATION TO CAUSATION: THE COST OF CORRUPTION

The data presented above show that good governance is strongly associated with development, but while corruption is strongly associated with underdevelopment, neither the scatterplots nor correlations analyses can provide any evidence as to whether development is not only associated with but also affected (caused or determined) by the level of corruption. We plan to show this in this section.

We noted earlier on that the CPI, for our dataset, has an average value of 4.5 and that varies from a minimum of 1.8 to a maximum of 9.4. In other words, one of the countries is perceived to be nearly free of corruption, while another is perceived to experience a very high level of corruption.

What is the price of corruption for the very corrupt country? And what would be the price that the virtually non-corrupt country would have to pay if the level of corruption in the country increased? In order to answer these questions, we need to perform regression analyses.[6] In the course of these analyses, corruption, measured on the basis of the CPI, is the independent variable, while the six measures of development discussed above are the response variables.

A regression analysis takes the form

$$Y = a + bX + e$$

where Y is the response variable, a is the intercept (the point where the regression line intercepts the y axis when $X = 0$) and e is the error term. Hence, if we substitute Y with one of the six measures of development, and we substitute CPI for X, we can assess how much change is reflected in literacy rate, employment in agriculture, GNI per capita, life expectancy, infant mortality, and number of motor vehicles as a result of a unit increase (or decrease) in CPI.

If we regress CPI against these six indicators of development, we find that corruption has a major impact on development no matter how the latter is measured and that some aspects of development are more deeply affected than others by levels of corruption. Further details are presented in Table 2.4.

Some analysts believe that R-squared only provides an indication of linearity, that is, of how a given change in the independent variable will be associated with a corresponding change in the dependent variable. Most, however, agree that the R-squared provides a clear indication of how much variance in the response variable is explained by the independent variable.

Following the latter approach, it can be seen from the fifth column in Table 2.4 that by regressing each of the measures of development against CPI, a sizeable portion of the variance in the response variable can be explained. Specifically, 23.6 percent of the variance in literacy rate, 34.3 percent of the variance in the level of employment in the agricultural sector, 39.8 percent of the variance in infant mortality rate, 50.4 percent of the variance in life expectancy, 53.8 percent in the variance of the number of motor vehicles, and 75.1 percent in the variance of GNI per capita can be explained by CPI.

But how much change does a unit increase in CPI induce in each of the response variables? The answer is provided in the third column of Table 2.4,

Table 2.4   Regression Analysis. Corruption and Development (sig.)

Y	A	B	X	R-squared
Literacy rate	66.259 (.000)	+4.950 (.001)	CPI	.236
Employment in agriculture	37.746 (.000)	−4.358 (.000)	CPI	.343
GNI per capita	−10834.46 (.000)	+4215.29 (.000)	CPI	.751
Life expectancy	56.244 (.000)	+3.143 (.000)	CPI	.504
Infant mortality rate	61.210 (.000)	−7.832 (.000)	CPI	.398
Motor vehicles	−84.436 (.151)	78.62 (.000)	CPI	.538

where we can see that a unit increase in CPI, which is a slight improvement in the level of transparency or a slight decline in the level of corruption, is responsible for a 3.14-year increase in life expectancy, a $4,215.29 increase in GNI per capita, a 4.358 percent decline in the level of employment in agriculture, a 4.95 percent increase in literacy rate, a 7.832 per thousand decline in infant mortality, and a 78.62 per thousand (or a 7.862 percent) increase in the number of vehicles.

In other words, a single unit decline in the level of perceived corruption is responsible for longer life, more wealth, more literacy, more cars, and more employment outside the agricultural sector.

Conversely, a single unit increase in the perceived corruption would induce a significant decline in the level of development regardless of how we measure it. This decline, simply put, is the cost of corruption, and it is the reason why it is essential to curb corruption in order to enable developing countries to enjoy sustainable growth and socio-economic development.

CONCLUSIONS

The purpose of this chapter was to show the costs of corruption and the dividends of good governance. After providing a brief overview of the literature on corruption, defining what is corruption and which contextual conditions favor the emergence of corruption, we paid attention to the impact that corruption has on development.

We did so by performing two sets of analysis. The first set showed that regardless of whether we measure development on the basis of literacy rate, GNI per capita, life expectancy, infant mortality, employment in agriculture, or number of motor vehicles, developed countries have lower levels of perceived corruption and poorer countries have higher levels. In fact, the analyses showed clearly that in less corrupt countries there is a higher literacy rate, a higher GNI per capita, longer life expectancy, lower infant mortality, more industrialization, and more motorization. By contrast, more corrupt countries are poorer, less industrialized, less educated, less motorized, and have a higher infant mortality rate and lower life expectancy. Both correlation analyses and scatterplots made clear that good governance is associated with development and that corruption is associated with underdevelopment.

The second set of analyses showed what the actual costs of corruption are and, conversely, the dividends of good governance. The regression analyses made clear that a unit improvement in corruption leads to higher income, more education, more industrialization, and so on, while a unit increase in corruption leads to lower income, less education, less industrialization, and so on. These analyses did not simply reveal that lower corruption leads to more development and that more corruption leads to more underdevelopment, but they also provided very specific indications of the costs of corruption and of the benefits of good governance.

These findings are very much consistent with the findings generated by Mauro (1997), Kaufmann (2000, 2006), Friedman at al. (2000), Hellman et al. (2000), and Johnson et al. (2003) and teach a simple lesson: that corruption is not simply bad in itself, it is bad for democracy, and, perhaps more importantly, bad for development.

In Chapter 3, we turn to the role that legislatures can play in curbing corruption.

NOTES

1. A particularly interesting line of research has investigated the relationship between democracy and development. Seminal was Lipset's article (1959), in which he reported that the number of developed countries that were democratic greatly outnumbered the number of countries that were developed and undemocratic. Lipset stated that socio-economic development is a necessary social requisite for the consolidation of democracy because "the more well-to-do a nation, the greater the chances that it will sustain democracy" (1959, p. 75). While his claim was fairly straightforward, other researchers went on to derive three different propositions from Lipset's main finding, that democracy is more likely to be found in richer countries—namely, that 1) developed countries are more likely to experience a transition to democracy than less developed countries; 2) that countries may undergo a democratic transition for a wide range of reasons, but democracy will survive only in richer countries; and 3) that democracy stimulates economic growth and development. Przeworski et al. (2000) were quick to note that while development has little impact on the probability that a country becomes democratic, it has a major impact on a whether a country is able to remain democratic. They noted that while a democratic regime has 12% probability of collapsing in a given year in countries where the income per capita is less than US $1,000, just 5.5% in countries with an income per capita of US $1,000–2,000, and virtually zero in countries with a per capita income of more than US $5,000. They also found that whether a regime is democratic or not has virtually no impact on the economic growth rate. In other words, democracy cannot be regarded as a major determinant of development.
2. While it is generally understood that "development" is a multifaceted phenomenon that entails social, economic, and political dimensions, it has been

acknowledged that social development, political development, and economic development do not occur at the same pace or speed. See Huntington (1968).

3. For example, economists such as Mises, Dietze (1963), and Hayek (1944, 1973) agree that any effort of the state to intervene in the economy will inevitably lead to economic inefficiency and ultimately, to economic failure. The new institutional economists, such as North (1990) and North and Thomas (1973), believe that economic development is a consequence of efficient economic organization and that the only task a state has to perform, in order to establish such an efficient economic organization, is to create the proper incentives (secure property rights) for the economic actors. Other scholars have shown that the state intervention in the economy can have a positive effect on the process of development. In the Russian case, Gerschenkron (1962) has demonstrated that the state assumed the role of the primary agent, propelling economic progress in the country. In East Asia, Wade (1990) has attributed the economic success of Japan and of the "Asian Tigers" to state intervention in the economy, while Katzenstein (1985) showed that the successful economic adaptation of the small European states to the changes in the global economy was favored by the cooperation between state and economic actors. Others, such as Peter Evans (1989, 1995), have argued that the important issue is whether the state is autonomous from social pressures and influences. According to Evans, the *predatory state* is characterized by the fact that it extracts resources from society and that it lacks the ability to prevent individuals from pursuing their own goals. Here, individual maximization of profits takes precedence over the pursuit of collective goals. In this type of state, ties to society are mostly ties to individuals: The state is not autonomous from society. This lack of state autonomy from societal pressures is the reason why state intervention in the economy does not foster development. The *developmental state*, by contrast, presides over the process of development and can promote development. Such states are characterized by "embedded autonomy"—they are internally organized on the basis of highly selective meritocratic criteria and by the presence of long-term career rewards. While it is beyond the purposes of the present book to discuss which of these analytical frameworks provides the best analytical tools for understanding socio-economic development, this brief overview of the role of the state in the economy testifies to the fact that scholars agree on the importance of economic development, but disagree on how it can be achieved.

4. In this regard, Urra (2007, p. 10) noted that Donchev and Ujhely (2007) reported that the correlation between CPI and the World Bank measure of corruption yielded a Pearson r coefficient of .98.

5. One of the authors performed a similar analysis with older data and with a smaller sample and found that socio-economic inequality, measured on the basis of the Gini coefficient, is strongly related to corruption. Specifically, it was found that corrupt societies are not just poorer but are also more unequal; on this see Pelizzo (2012). Pelizzo and Stapenhurst (2007), in their analysis of the impact of good governance and corruption on various measures of development in Africa, also found that corruption is detrimental to development.

6. Regression analyses are statistical analyses that tell how much change is induced (caused) in the response variable by a unit change in the independent variable (cause), whether the induced change is significant both in substantive and statistical terms, and how much change in the response variable is explained or can be explained by changes in the independent variable.

REFERENCES

Dietze, G. (1963). *In Defense of Property*. Chicago: Regnery.
Donchev, D., and G. Ujhely. (2007). Do Corruption Indices Measure Corruption? Working paper, Economics Department, Harvard University, March 25.

Evans, P. (1989). Predatory, Developmental, and Other Apparatuses: A Comparative Political Economy Perspective on the Third World State. *Sociological Forum*, 4(4), 561–587.

Evans, P. (1995). *Embedded Autonomy*. Princeton: Princeton UP.

Friedman, E., S. Johnson, D. Kaufmann, and P. Zoido-Lobaton. (2000). Dodging the Grabbing Hand: The Determinants of Unofficial Activity in 69 Countries. *Journal of Public Economics*, 76, 459–493.

Gerschenkron, A. (1962). *Economic Backwardness in Historical Perspective*. Cambridge: Belknap Press of Harvard UP.

Hayek, F. (1944). *The Road to Serfdom*. Chicago: Chicago UP.

Hayek, F. (1973). *Law, Legislation and Liberty*. Chicago: Chicago UP.

Hellman, J.S., G. Jones, D. Kaufmann, and P. Zoido-Lobaton. (2000). Seize the State, Seize the Day—An Empirical Analysis of State Capture and Corruption in Transition. *World Bank Policy Research Working Paper*, no. 2444, September.

Huntington, S. (1968). *Political Order in Changing Societies*. New Haven: Yale UP.

Huntington, S. (1991). *The Third Wave of Democratization*. Norman: University of Oklahoma Press.

Johnson, S., D. Kaufmann, J. McMillan, and C. Woodruff. (2003). Why Do Firms Hide? Bribes and Unofficial Activity after Communism. *Public Economics Econ-WPA* 0308004. Washington, D.C.: World Bank.

Katzenstein, P. (1985). *Small States in World Markets*. Ithaca: Cornell UP.

Kaufmann, D. (2000). Governance and Anti-Corruption. In V. Thomas et al. *The Quality of Growth*. New York: Oxford University Press.

Kaufmann, D. (2006). Myths and Realities of Governance and Corruption. *The World Economic Forum Global Competitiveness Report 2005–6*. New York: World Economic Forum.

Lipset, S.M. (1959). Some Social Requisites of Democracy. *American Political Science Review*, LIII(1), 69–105.

Mauro, P. (1997). The Effects of Corruption on Growth, Investment and Government Expenditure: A Cross Country Analysis. In K.A. Ellio (Ed.) *Corruption and the Global Economy*, pp. 83–107. Washington, D.C.: Institute for International Economics.

Murphy, K.M., A. Shleifer, and R.W. Vishny. (1991). The Allocation of Talent: Implications for Growth. *The Quarterly Journal of Economics*, 106, 503–30.

North, D. (1990). *Institutions, Institutional Change and Economic Performance*. Cambridge: Cambridge UP.

North, D., and R.P. Thomas. (1973). *The Rise of the Western World*. Cambridge: Cambridge UP.

Pelizzo, R. (2012). *Le Strategie Della Crescita. Saggi di Politica Economica*. Napoli: Guida.

Pelizzo, R., and R. Stapenhurst. (2007). The Role of Parliament in Promoting Good Governance in Africa (September 18, 2007). Available at: SSRN: http://ssrn.com/abstract=2101133

Pelizzo, R., and R. Stapenhurst. (2012). *Parliamentary Oversight Tools*. London: Routledge.

Przeworski, A., M.E. Alvarez, J.A. Cheibub and F. Limongi(2000). *Democracy and Development*. New York: Cambridge University Press.

Tanzi, V., and H. Davoodi. (1997). Corruption, Public Investment, and Growth. *IMF Working Paper* 97/139.

Urra, F.J. (2007). Assessing Corruption. An Analytical Review of Corruption Measurement and its Problems: Perception, Error and Utility. Working Paper, Edmund A. Walsch School of Foreign Affairs, Georgetown University, May.

Wade, R. (1990). *Governing the Market*. Princeton: Princeton UP.

Wei, S-J., and D. Kaufmann. (1998). Does "Grease Money" Speed Up the Wheels of Commerce? *International Monetary Fund* (Washington, D.C.). Available at: www.imf.org/external/pubs/cat/longres.cfm?sk=3524.0

World Bank. (1997). *World Development Report: The Art of the State*. Washington, D.C.

3   Strategies to Curb Corruption—The Role of the Legislature

INTRODUCTION

We saw in Chapter 1 that there are several types of corruption (bureaucratic, grand, and legislative) and that the strategies to curb corruption are multi-dimensional and multi-stakeholder, with one of the principal, but so far largely neglected, stakeholders being the legislature. This is surprising, since each of the core functions of parliaments—legislation/policy making, representation, and oversight—has an important role in the control of corruption. In this chapter, we will examine each of these legislative functions and how they can contribute to reduced corruption.

The evidence consistently shows that the establishment of systems of accountability is crucial for curbing corruption. As we have discussed elsewhere (Stapenhurst, Pelizzo, and Jacobs, 2013; Pelizzo and Stapenhurst, 2012), a political system in which government officials must account for their actions, for their expenses, and for their decisions is less likely to be corrupt. There is a simple reason why systems of accountability deter corruption—in a political system where government officials need to explain why they do what they do, the probability of being caught for engaging in corrupt or unethical practices is higher and the returns are lower—hence individuals have fewer economic incentives for being corrupt.

The international community has long emphasized that legislatures, which act as agents of the electorate, have a clear mandate to oversee the actions and the expenditures of the executive, and they are hence an integral part of any system of accountability. In contemporary political systems, the oversight function is the single most important function a legislature can perform. In recent years, new modes of representation have emerged and new forms of political expression have appeared. Citizens—with the technology revolution, with Internet and so on—have found a variety of new ways for making their voices heard. Hence, while legislatures still perform a representative function, the importance of performing this function has somewhat diminished. Similarly, because of the knowledge gap between the executive and the legislative branch, it has come to be accepted that the executive branch has the prerogative to initiate the legislative, in the sense of law-making, process. Hence, while legislatures still perform an enormously important legislative function, the importance of performing this function has somewhat declined. The decline in the importance of performing these two functions has been coupled with an increase in the importance of performing the oversight function. It is precisely because the legislature has lost some of its influence in the legislative process that it has to be even more effective in overseeing policy and budget implementation.

But while the promotion of legislatures with greater oversight capacity has been a staple of any successful anti-corruption strategy for nearly 20 years, the international community has also been aware of the fact that stronger legislatures are a necessary but insufficient condition for curbing corruption. The success of any anti-corruption strategy requires a lot more than effective legislative oversight. It also requires that legislatures function properly, that the behavior of legislatures and legislators is ethical, and that the selection of candidates or the electoral process is not vitiated or affected by corrupt practices. Hence, while it is crucially important that legislatures are properly equipped to perform their oversight function, there must be also additional regulations to prevent, minimize, and possibly eliminate the instances of electoral corruption, electoral fraud, and unethical behavior.

In this chapter, we review the different types of corruption—bureaucratic, grand, and legislative—presented previously in Chapter 1 and consider the corresponding set of legislative mechanisms available to help control those types of corruption. In subsequent chapters, we examine other types of legislative corruption (unethical behavior by legislators, electoral fraud, and political finance) and consider how such corruption can be reduced.

TAXONOMY OF CORRUPTION AND LEGISLATIVE OVERSIGHT TOOLS

As we noted in Chapter 1, Jain (2001) differentiated between three types of corruption (see Figure 3.1). Bureaucratic corruption refers to distortions in implementing such laws, policies, and regulations. In its most common form, civil servants demand small bribes from the public to receive a service to which they are entitled, receive a service to which they are not entitled, or simply to speed up a bureaucratic procedure. By contrast, grand corruption usually involves political leaders, the latter being defined by Jain (2001, p. 105) as those "... that [have] worked out an equilibrium relationship [with their] constituents and [are] able to make and implement economic and political decisions." As elected officials, such leaders are expected to make economic and financial decisions that further the interests of their principals—the citizens who elected them. Corrupt leaders can change national policies to serve their own interests, at some cost to citizens. He further argued that grand corruption refers to distortions in the *formulation* of laws, policies, and regulations while bureaucratic corruption refers to distortions in *implementation* of such laws, policies, and regulations. (We consider legislative corruption in Chapter 5).

Electoral corruption is an obvious subcategory of grand corruption. Electoral corruption occurs whenever politicians—and more specifically political candidates—engage in one of the following two sets of activities. The electoral process can be corrupted in two basic ways, depending on whether the politician or the candidate plays an active or a passive role in the corrupt transaction. An electoral campaign can be corrupted whenever a candidate accepts contributions to his/her campaign in violation of the electoral and political finance legislation. For instance, the candidate may violate the law by accepting contributions from sources that are banned from contributing to electoral and campaign finance, by accepting contributions in excess of the limits established by the electoral finance legislation, by accepting contributions to serve the interests of the donors if elected, and so on (see Chapter 5 for further details). But while in each of these scenarios, the politician or the candidate plays a passive role as he/she is the recipient of a corrupt transaction, there are also several instances in which the candidate plays an active role. For example, the candidate may violate the limits on electoral expenses established by the campaign finance legislation or, in the most extreme case, he/she may even buy votes.

There are various institutional solutions that have been devised to cope with electoral corruption. Anti-corruption agencies, electoral commissions, and legislative and normative dispositions, along with specific parliamentary committees have been created, adopted, and developed to minimize the incidence of this type of corruption. For all the other manifestations of bureaucratic and grand corruption, legislatures have developed a number of mechanisms or tools. These are summarized in Table 3.1.

Legislatures usually address corruption while performing their oversight function which, along with the representative and the legislative, is one of the three fundamental functions performed by legislatures worldwide. The literature has categorized the tools of legislative oversight in a variety of

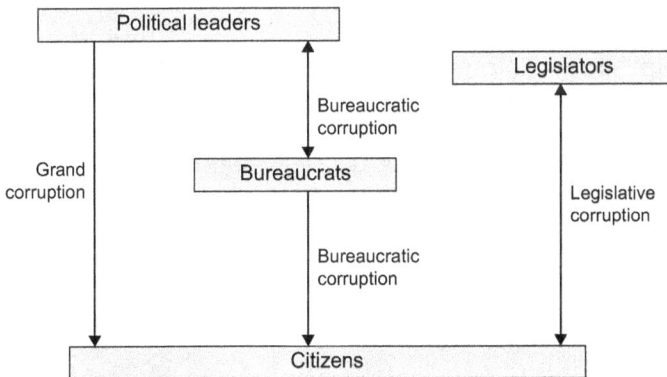

Figure 3.1   Types of Corruption

Source: Jain (2001)

Table 3.1   Taxonomy of Corruption—and Legislative Oversight Tools

Type of corruption	Examples	Legislative oversight tools
Bureaucratic	Bribery—usually "petty" Nepotism Misappropriation Extortion Influence peddling Speed money Embezzlement	Committees Supreme audit institution Anti-corruption agency Ombudsperson

Political–Executive	Bribery—often "grand"
	 State capture
	 Nepotism
	 Misappropriation
	 Adoption of laws/
	    regulations that favor
	    one group/person
	 Influence peddling
	 Embezzlement
		Committees
		 Special inquiries
		 Questions
		 Interpellations
		 No confidence/censure/
		    impeachment
		 Supreme audit institution
		 Anti-corruption agency
		 Executive codes of conduct
		    recall

ways. For instance, Maffio (2002) paid attention to whether they employed ex ante or ex post; other taxonomic efforts have paid attention to whether they are used by individual Members of Parliament (MPs) or by the legislature as a whole, to the effectiveness or the bite of such tools (Maffio, 2002; Stapenhurst, Jacobs, and Pelizzo, 2014; Stapenhurst, Pelizzo, and Jacobs, 2013). In this chapter, following the approach adopted by Pelizzo and Stapenhurst (2012), we do not map tools or capacity on the basis of those criteria, but on the basis of the type of corruption that they are best suited to monitor and detect. Hence, committee hearings, supreme audit institutions, ombudspersons, and anti-corruption agencies are the best suited tools to cope with bureaucratic corruption. While some of these tools (hearings, Supreme Audit Institutions (SAIs), anti-corruption agencies) may also play a role in coping with political corruption, the evidence suggests that this type of corruption is also effectively tackled by legislative overseers through the use of questions, interpellations, motions, the administration of executive codes of conduct, or a combination of such tools.

SOME EMPIRICAL FINDINGS

Despite the wealth of information generated by the study of legislative oversight with regard to the virtues, the tools, and the conditions of effective oversight, much less has been written with regard to the impact of oversight, including on corruption.

Research has noted that the presence of the oversight tools is a necessary but insufficient condition for oversight. Effective oversight depends not only on the availability of mechanisms, but depends also on additional conditions, including whether the parliament has the ability to modify legislation (Loewenberg and Patterson, 1979), whether parliaments and parliamentarians are given proper information to perform their oversight tasks adequately (Frantzich, 1979; Jewell, 1978), swings in the political mood of the country (Ogul and Rockman, 1990), tensions between the executive and the legislative, the saliency of issues, and how aggressively the opposition performs its role (Rockman, 1984; Maor, 1999). But a key question remains: Does legislative oversight help curb corruption?

As oversight potential increases, it becomes easier to scrutinize and control the government and its activities, and, since controlling the government is a key component of anti-corruption strategies, the more a government is subject to potential control, the more likely it is for the corruption to be reduced. In other words, oversight potential is a cause of lower corruption. Having hypothesized this possible causal relationship, it is necessary to test whether there is any empirical evidence sustaining the claim that the probability that a country has lower levels of corruption increases as the oversight potential increases.

The Data

The Inter-Parliamentary Union (IPU), in collaboration with the World Bank Institute (WBI), conducted a survey in 2009 of its 120 members on Executive–Legislative relations. Over 90 legislatures responded, giving a response rate of 78 percent.

Respondents were asked several questions: whether the administration in their country was "considered an institution that must report to Parliament," "how does the parliament exercise oversight?", "whether parliamentarians could question government officials," "whether question time was allocated," "whether interpellations were foreseen," and, finally, "whether there was an ombudsman in the country." See Table 3.2.

Findings

The findings provide interesting information. First, they indicate that there is considerable variation in how common these various tools of oversight are (see Table 3.3). For example, legislators can put oral or written questions to the government in 69 of the 94 responding countries; similarly, committees of inquiry and committee hearings are also common, utilized in 87 countries. By contrast, motions for debate and missions to government departments concerned are substantially less common, with motions used in 62 countries and missions to government departments in 35 countries.

As a proxy for national levels of corruption, the 2012 ranking of countries by Transparency International (TI) was used. As noted in Chapter 2, the index is measured on a 10-point scale, where 0 indicates highly corrupt and 10 indicates highly honest (see Table 3.4).

Table 3.2 Countries and the Number of Parliamentary Oversight Tools

			Number of oversight tools			
2	3	4	5	6	7	8
Cambodia	Côte d'Ivoire	Cameroon	Algeria	Andorra	Antigua & Barbuda	Bangladesh
Qatar		Chile	Bahrain	Argentina	Austria	Burkina Faso
Tajikistan		Turkey	Bhutan	Armenia	Benin	Congo, Dem. Rep
Uganda		Yemen	Canada	Bulgaria	Costa Rica	Czech Republic
			Central African Rep.	Burundi	Djibouti	Jamaica
			Croatia	Estonia	Finland	Jordan
			Cyprus	France	Gabon	Kenya
			Germany	Grenada	Georgia	Liechtenstein
			Ghana	Indonesia	Greece	Lithuania
			Iceland	Ireland	Haiti	Morocco
			Israel	Liberia	Hungary	Namibia
			Japan	New Zealand	Iran	Sweden
			Korea, Rep. of	Norway	Latvia	Tanzania
			Lebanon	Paraguay	Malaysia	Tonga
			Lesotho	Romania	Netherlands	Ukraine
			Luxembourg	San Marino	Poland	Uruguay
			Macedonia	Singapore	Senegal	Vietnam
			Marshall Islands	Slovakia	Serbia	
			Maurituis	Sri Lanka	Slovenia	
			Moldova	Trinidad & Tobago	Spain	
			Nicaragua	Tunisia	Switzerland	
			Palau	U.K.	Zimbabwe	
			Philippines			
			Seychelles			
			Thailand			
			Togo			

Table 3.3 How Common Are These Oversight Tools? (Number of Countries)

Committee hearing	Motions for debate	Committee of inquiry	Oral & written questions	Missions to govt. depts.	Interpell-ations	Ombuds	Reports
87	62	81	89	63	68	74	67

Table 3.4 Transparency International—Corruption Perception Index (2012)

Finland 9.0	Saint Vincent 6.2	South Africa 4.3	Armenia 3.4	Nigeria 2.7
Denmark 9.0	Slovenia 6.1	Bosnia + Herzegovina 4.2	Bolivia 3.4	Pakistan 2.7
New Zealand 9.0	Taiwan 6.1	Italy 4.2	Gambia 3.4	Bangladesh 2.6
Sweden 8.8	Cape Verde 6.0	Sao Tome + Principe 4.2	Kosovo 3.4	Cameroon 2.6
Singapore 8.7	Israel 6.0	Bulgaria 4.1	Mali 3.4	Central African Republic 2.6
Switzerland 8.6	Dominica 5.8	Liberia 4.1	Mexico 3.4	Congo Rep. 2.6
Australia 8.5	Poland 5.8	Montenegro 4.1	Philippines 3.4	Syria 2.6
Norway 8.5	Malta 5.7	Tunisia 4.1	Albania 3.3	Ukraine 2.6
Canada 8.4	Mauritius 5.7	Sri Lanka 4.0	Ethiopia 3.3	Eritrea 2.5
Netherlands 8.4	South Korea 5.6	China 3.9	Guatemala 3.3	Guinea-Bissau 2.5
Iceland 8.2	Brunei 5.5	Serbia 3.9	Niger 3.3	PNG 2.5
Luxembourg 8.0	Hungary 5.5	Trinidad + Tobago 3.9	Timor Leste 3.3	Paraguay 2.5
Germany 7.9	Costa Rica 5.4	Burkina Faso 3.8	Dominican Republic 3.2	Guinea 2.4
Hong Kong 7.7	Lithuania 5.4	El Salvador 3.8	Ecuador 3.2	Krgyz Rep. 2.4
Barbados 7.6	Rwanda 5.3	Jamaica 3.8	Egypt 3.2	Yemen 2.3
Belgium 7.5	Georgia 5.2	Panama 3.8	Indonesia 3.2	Angola 2.2
Japan 7.4	Seychelles 5.2	Peru 3.8	Madagascar 3.2	Cambodia 2.2

(Continued)

Table 3.4 (Continued)

United Kingdom 7.4	Bahrain 5.1	Malawi 3.7	Belarus 3.1	Tajikistan 2.2
USA 7.3	Czech Rep. 4.9	Morocco 3.7	Mauritania 3.1	DRC 2.1
Chile 7.2	Latvia 4.9	Suriname 3.7	Mozambique 3.1	Laos 2.1
Uruguay 7.2	Malaysia 4.9	Swaziland 3.7	Sierra Leone 3.1	Libya 2.1
Bahamas 7.1	Turkey 4.9	Thailand 3.7	Vietnam 3.1	Eq. Guinea 2.0
France 7.1	Cuba 4.8	Zambia 3.7	Lebanon 3.0	Zimbabwe 2.0
St. Lucia 7.1	Jordan 4.8	Benin 3.7	Togo 2.9	Burundi 1.9
Austria 6.9	Namibia 4.8	Colombia 3.6	Cote d'Ivoire 2.9	Chad 1.9
Ireland 6.9	Oman 4.7	Djibouti 3.6	Nicaragua 2.9	Haiti 1.8
Qatar 6.8	Croatia 4.6	Greece 3.6	Uganda 2.9	Venezuela 1.9
UAE 6.8	Slovakia 4.6	India 3.6	Comoros 2.8	Iraq 1.8
Cyprus 6.6	Ghana 4.5	Moldova 3.6	Guyana 2.8	Turkmen-Istan 1.7
Botswana 6.5	Lesotho 4.5	Mongolia 3.6	Honduras 2.8	Uzbekistan 1.7
Spain 6.5	Kuwait 4.4	Senegal 3.6	Iran 2.8	Myanmar 1.5
Estonia 6.4	Saudi Arabia 4.4	Argentina 3.5	Kazahkstan 2.8	Sudan 1.3
Bhutan 6.3	Romania 4.4	Gabon 3.5	Russia 2.8	Afghanistan 0.8
Portugal 6.3	Brazil 4.3	Tanzania 3.5	Azerbaijan 2.7	North Korea 0.8
Puerto Rico 6.3	Macedonia 4.3	Algeria 3.4	Kenya 2.7	Somalia 0.8

Given the nature of the data, it is not possible to test whether legislative oversight is effective in reducing corruption for three reasons. First, the data (concerning the number of oversight tools available to a given legislature) provide a fairly clear indication of a parliament's potential, but they provide no indication of whether such oversight is performed effectively. Second, TI's CPI only measures perceived levels of corruption. This means that some countries and political systems are perceived to be more corrupt than others in spite of the fact that they may be less corrupt in objective terms. Moreover, the TI data are rather "blunt," as they aggregate all types of corruption. Third, correlation analysis shows association and does not show causation. With these caveats in mind, the next section tests whether the level of perceived wrongdoing is related to, and possibly affected by, the number of oversight mechanisms available to the parliament, that is, to the parliament's oversight potential.

Discussion

Table 3.5 shows that there is not a strong correlation between countries with more oversight tools and levels of perceived corruption. This is in sharp contrast with earlier data (Stapenhurst, Pelizzo, and Jacobs, forthcoming), which showed a stronger correlation. Indeed, the data presented in Tabl 3.6 show that when we regress the CPI against the number of oversight tools, we find that the regression coefficient is negative and insignificant and that the regression model explains 0% in the variance of corruption. We need to find alternative explanations, one of which is a country's form of government.

Form of Government
Previous research has indicated that legislatures operating within parliamentary forms of government have greater oversight than those operating in semi-presidential and presidential systems (Gerring and Thacker, 2004; Lederman et al., 2005; Pelizzo and Stapenhurst, 2008). However, evidence supporting these studies could be spurious. It might be that the analysis is capturing not so much the relationship between oversight potential and perceived corruption, but rather the fact that the level of perceived corruption is related to, and arguably affected by, the form of government (i.e., the extension of the Lederman et al. [2005] argument).

When we regress CPI against the form of government, we find that the form of government has a strong, significant, and negative impact on the CPI. A word of explanation is at this point in order. In our analysis, the form of government variable is a trichotomous variable that assumes a value of 1 for countries that are parliamentary, 2 for semi-presidential countries, and 3 for countries that are presidential. The fact that this trichotomous variable has a negative effect on the level of CPI means that its impact on the level of transparency is highest in parliamentary systems, lowest in presidential

Table 3.5 Oversight Tools and Perceived Corruption

	Number of oversight tools						
CPI range	2	3	4	5	6	7	8
0–1.9					Burundi	Haiti	
2.0–3.9	Cambodia Tajikistan Uganda	Cameroon Côte d'Ivoire	Yemen	Algeria Central African Rep, Lebanon Moldova Nicaragua Philippines Thailand Togo	Argentina Armenia Indonesia Paraguay Trinidad + Tobago	Benin Djibouti Gabon Greece Senegal Serbia Zimbabwe	Bangladesh Burkina Faso Congo, Dem. Rep Jamaica Kenya Morocco Tanzania Ukraine Vietnam
4.0–5.9			Turkey	Bahrain Croatia Ghana Korea, Rep. of Lesotho Macedonia Maurituis Seychelles	Bulgaria Georgia Liberia Romania Slovakia Sri Lanka Tunisia	Costa Rica Latvia Malaysia Poland	Czech Rep. Jordan Lithuania Namibia

6.0–7.9	Qatar	Chile	Bhutan Cyprus Germany Israel Japan	Estonia France Ireland U.K.	Austria Spain	Uruguay
8–10			Canada Iceland Luxembourg	New Zealand Norway Singapore	Finland Netherlands Switzerland	Sweden

Note: TI did not rank Andorra, Antigua & Barbuda, Grenada, Liechtenstein, Marshall Islands, Palau, San Marino, or Tonga.

Table 3.6   Perceived Corruption, Oversight Potential, and Form of Government

Dependent variable	Intercept	Number of oversight tools	Form of government	Missions to government	R-squared
CPI	4.578 (.000)	−.010 (.949)			.000
CPI	6.440 (.000)		−1.073 (.000)		.168
CPI	6.966 (.000)	−.082 (.588)	−1.093 (.000)		.171
CPI	6.944 (.000)		−1.073 (.000)	−1.260 (005)	.245

systems, and in-between for semi-presidential systems. This model explains nearly 17 percent (16.8%) in the variance of CPI. When we regress CPI against the number of oversight tools *and* the form of government, our explanatory power does not improve much: It increases from 16.8 percent to 17.1 percent. The regression coefficient for the number of oversight tools is weak, negative, and statistically insignificant, whereas the coefficient for the form of government is strong, significant, and negative. In other words, when we control for the impact of the form of government, the impact of the number of oversight tools on CPI remains insignificant. Whereas when we control for the impact of the number of oversight tools, the impact of the form of government on CPI remains strong and significant.

Why does the number of oversight tools have no influence on the level of corruption in a given country? Several explanations have been posited. Some studies (e.g., Pelizzo and Stapenhurst, 2012) have shown that the level of corruption in given country, just like the quality of democracy, is affected by the effectiveness with which oversight tools are employed, rather than by the number of tools a legislature could employ. Other studies (Stapenhurst, 2011; Pelizzo and Stapenhurst, 2013) have argued that the number of oversight tools at the disposal of a legislature is not necessarily the best way to measure the oversight capacity of a legislature. Stapenhurst (2011) advanced the notion that that oversight effectiveness and the ability to curb corruption are a function of oversight capacity but that such capacity should be assessed by taking into consideration not only the internal oversight tools (questions, interpellations, hearings), but also the external ones (such as supreme audit institutions, anti-corruption agencies), facilitating conditions (size of supporting staff, research facilities) and the socio-political context (executive-political relations, access to information, public trust in parliament) within which the legislature operates. Pelizzo and Stapenhurst (2013) have shown that when oversight capacity is measured by taking into consideration these three sets of factors, it has a significant impact not only on

Table 3.7 Correlation Analysis, Oversight Tools, and Perceived Corruption

	CPI
Written and oral questions	.227 (.036)
Interpellations	–.166 (.128)
Motions for debate	.003 (.980)
Hearings in committee	.175 (.106)
Committees of inquiry	.129 (.236)
Missions	–.262 (015)
Reports	.142 (.192)
Ombudsman	–.047 (.668)

the effectiveness with which oversight is exercised but also on quality of democracy and level of good governance.

It is important to note that not all oversight tools are equal in their effectiveness. The correlation and gamma correlations presented in Tables 3.7 and 3.8 sustain the claim that measurement of oversight capacity is imperfect and that simply counting the number of oversight tools is not the optimal way to do so.[1] Both sets of correlation show that the there are three broad types of oversight tools: those that have no significant impact on CPI, those that have a positive and significant impact on CPI, and those that have a positive and negative impact on CPI. If we add them all together, the variables that have a significant impact may cancel each other out, and as a result, the number of oversight tools will appear to be unrelated to CPI.

But while the number of oversight tools, measured as an additive scale, is not significantly related to CPI, legislative oversight and legislative oversight tools are indeed related to CPI. This conclusion is supported not only by the correlation and the gamma correlation analyses, but also by the regression analyses presented in Table 3.6. In fact, when we regress CPI against form of government and legislative missions, we explain nearly a quarter in the variance of CPI; both variables have a strong, negative, and significant impact on the level of good governance. Corruption is higher in countries where missions are one of the oversight tools at the disposal of the legislature; corruption increases as the political system becomes more presidentialized.

Table 3.8 Gamma Correlation Analysis, Oversight Tools, and Perceived Corruption

	CPI
Written and oral questions	.657
	(−026)
Interpellations	−.173
	(.365)
Motions for debate	.028
	(.835)
Hearings in committee	.455
	(.078)
Committees of inquiry	.188
	(.264)
Missions	−.268
	(.027)
Reports	.215
	(.126)
Ombudsman	−.038
	(.828)

CONCLUSIONS

In this chapter, we have built on the differentiation of different types of corruption identified by Jain (2001) and have considered the role of the legislature in curbing corruption. We presented a taxonomy that suggests different legislative oversight tools are useful in combating different types of corruption, and have undertaken some empirical analyses. The results of our analyses both confirm and go beyond that of Lederman et al. (2005): They show that presidential forms of government are associated with higher levels of corruption than are non-presidential forms of government, and also that countries with semi-presidential forms of government fall in-between. In other words, ". . . parliamentary systems [along with democracy, political stability, and freedom of the press] . . . are associated with lower corruption (Lederman et al., 2005, p. 28). The reason for this is that factors of the ". . . political macrostructure determine the incentives for those in office to be honest and police and punish misbehavior of people inside and outside the government bureaucracy" (Lederman et al., 2005, p. 37).

But our analysis goes further, to reach a very different conclusion. The incentive for office holders are shaped not so much by macrostructures, but rather by meso-level institutions, such as the oversight tools, facilitating factors that support the oversight function and contextual factors such as the form of government. At the same time, we go beyond our simpler analyses

(Stapenhurst and Pelizzo, 2013), which posited that it was the number of oversight tools that determined oversight capacity and propose a more nuanced framework.

Our analysis suggests some new considerations about meso-level institutions. First, the importance of oversight tools is less than originally thought, is conditional, and varies across forms of government. Moreover, not all oversight tools are equally effective, and what works for some forms of government may not work well, or at all, in other systems. Hence, these findings underline that the "one size fits all" approach is inadequate when it comes to strengthening legislative capacity and curbing corruption.

Second, we have learned that facilitating conditions, such as the size of legislative libraries and of parliamentary research staff, are important—as are the factors such as trust in parliament, which shape the environment within which legislatures operate. And, perhaps even more important, it is not just the simple existence of oversight tools, facilitating factors or even contextual factors that determine oversight effectiveness—and hence, lower levels of corruption—but rather the political will of legislators to exercise their oversight function. We turn to this issue in the next chapter.

NOTE

1. A correlation measures the strength and the direction of a (linear) relationship between two variables. The gamma correlation measures the strength of the association of two variables measured at the ordinal level.

REFERENCES

Frantzich, S. E. (1979). Computerized Information Technology in the US House of Representatives. *Legislative Studies Quarterly*, 4(2), 255–280.

Gerring, J., and S Thacker, S. (2004). Political Institutions and Corruption: The Role of Unitism and Parliamentarism. *British Journal of Political Science*, 34, 295–330.

Jain, A. K. (2001). *Political Economy of Corruption* London: Routledge.

Jewell, M. E. (1978). Legislative Studies in Western Democracies: A Comparative Analysis *Legislative Studies Quarterly*, 3(4), 537–554.

Lederman, D., N. Loayza, and R. Soares. (2005). Accountability and Corruption: Political Institutions Do Matter. *Economics and Politics*, 17 (March), 1–35.

Loewenberg, G., and S. C. Patterson. (1979). *Comparing Legislatures*. Boston, MA: Little, Brown and Co.

Maffio, R. (2002). Quis Custodiet Ipsos Custodes? Il Controllo Parlamentare Dell'attivita' di Governo in Prospettiva Comparata. *Quaderni di Scienza Politica*, 9(2), 333–383.

Maor, M. (1999). Electoral Competition and the Oversight Game: A Transaction Cost Approach and the Norwegian Experience. *European Journal of Political Research*, 35, 371–388.

Ogul, M., and B. Rockman (1990). Overseeing Oversight: New Departures and Old Problems. *Legislative Studies Quarterly,* 15(1), 5–24.

Pelizzo, R., and R. Stapenhurst. (2008). Tools for Legislative Oversight: An Empirical Investigation. In R. Stapenhurst, R. Pelizzo, D. Olson, and L. von Trapp (Eds.) *Legislative Oversight and Budgeting: A World Perspective.* Washington D.C.: The World Bank Institute.

Pelizzo R., and R. Stapenhurst. (2012). *Parliamentary Oversight Tools.* London: Routledge.

Pelizzo R., and R. Stapenhurst. (2013). *Government Accountability and Legislative Oversight.* New York: Routledge.

Rockman, B. A. (1984). Legislative—Executive Relations and Legislative Oversight. *Legislative Studies Quarterly,* 9(3), 387–440.

Stapenhurst, Frederick (Rick). (2011). *Legislative Oversight and Curbing Corruption; Presidentialism and Parliamentarianism Revisited.* Unpublished PhD thesis. Canberra: Australian National University.

Stapenhurst, Frederick, Kerry Jacobs, and Riccardo Pelizzo. (2014). The Role of Legislatures in Curbing Corruption. *Public Integrity,* 16(3), 285–304.

Stapenhurst, Frederick, Riccardo Pelizzo, and K. Jacobs. (2013). *Following the Money.* London: Pluto Press.

4 The Effectiveness of Legislative Oversight

The Case of Ghana and Nigeria in Comparative Perspective

INTRODUCTION

In the previous chapters, we touched on some of the most important themes of this book. In Chapter 2 we showed that corruption has a detrimental effect on economic growth and development, and that both developed and developing countries may enjoy the dividends of good governance if they just manage to reduce corruption. In Chapter 3, we discussed the role of parliament in curbing corruption. Specifically, building on some of our previous work (Pelizzo and Stapenhurst, 2013), we pointed out that legislatures perform representative, legislative, and oversight functions and that the effectiveness with which legislatures perform their oversight function depends on the number and type of both internal and external oversight tools (where committees, question periods, and debates in plenary are examples of the former, and supreme audit institutions and ombud offices are examples of the latter), on facilitating conditions such as the size of the parliamentary library and the number of research staff, and on contextual factors such as public trust in parliament and form of government.

This finding is consistent with earlier findings. Pelizzo and Stapenhurst (2012) showed that oversight effectiveness leads to the better functioning of a political system, a higher democratic quality, and less corruption. Stapenhurst, Pelizzo, and Jacobs (2013), in their global analysis of Public Accounts Committees (PACs), reported that where such committees are more active and effective, there is a marked decline in the level of corruption.

Hence, the first lesson so far is that legislatures do play a role in curbing corruption by performing their oversight function. Or, to articulate the same idea in a slightly different way, when legislatures effectively perform their oversight function, they make a significant contribution to both preventing and detecting corruption.

As we will see later in this chapter and, in more in detail, in Chapter 5, the ability and willingness of parliaments to curb corruption contributes to the effectiveness with which the oversight function is performed and makes a significant contribution to the legitimacy of the parliament as an institution and to the legitimacy of the political system as a whole.

Before turning our attention to the relationship between oversight effectiveness, political willingness to curb corruption, and legitimacy, or to what institutional devices can be adopted to increase willingness of parliaments to perform their role in fighting corruption, we first pay attention to the conditions that are responsible for the effectiveness of legislative oversight. We do so by performing an in-depth comparative analysis of Ghana and Nigeria, and we will use this comparative analysis to set up the stage for the analyses presented in the rest of the book.

In this chapter, we proceed as follows. In the first section, in addition to justifying why we decided to focus our attention on the cases of Ghana and Nigeria, we provide a short but fairly comprehensive picture of the political, institutional, and contextual conditions within which the legislatures of Ghana and Nigeria operate. In the second section, we present some evidence that we have gathered in the course of field research to assess the effectiveness of legislative oversight in both countries and legislatures' ability to curb corruption.[1] In so doing, we address a theme that will be discussed in greater detail in the following chapters, namely that in some settings, lack of public legitimacy and perceived corruption prevent legislatures from effectively performing their oversight task functions and from effectively fighting corruption. We will show that legislatures need to take proactive steps (such as adopting Codes of Conduct) to regain citizen trust and to reduce instances of legislative corruption (see Chapter 6). In the third section, we will show the extent to which the legitimacy of parliament is deeply tainted and damaged by its perceived corruption. In the final section, we will draw some tentative conclusions.

SETTING THE STAGE: GHANA AND NIGERIA IN COMPARATIVE PERSPECTIVE

Ghana and Nigeria are good cases to be included in an in-depth comparative analysis. They are both located in West Africa, they share a similar colonial legacy, they both have experienced extensive constitutional instability in the wake of national independence, they both have a first-past-the-post (FPTP) electoral system, they have roughly the same GDP per capita ($1,000 in Ghana, $1,400 in Nigeria), and they both experience considerable ethnic fragmentation, with over 100 distinct ethnic groups in Ghana and more than 250 in Nigeria. Furthermore, neither country has a parliamentary form of government: Nigeria has a presidential form and Ghana a semi-presidential system. These similarities should not make us overlook the fact that the countries also display significant differences: Ghana has a unitary form of state, while Nigeria has a federal one; Ghana is geographically smaller and significantly less populated than Nigeria; and the parliament of Ghana is unicameral, while the Nigerian one is bicameral.

These characteristics pertain to a very general or macro level such as form of government, form of state, electoral system, and demographic characteristics. Several years ago, in one of their initial analyses of the relationship between legislative oversight and the quality of democracy, Pelizzo and Stapenhurst (2006) argued that in order to understand why democracy survives in some settings but not in others and indeed why it works better in some countries than it does in others, it was necessary to shift the focus of analysis from general, macro-level characteristics to medium or meso-level characteristics. In other words, they suggested that in order to understand the functioning of a political system or of an institution, it was necessary to look not only at its most general characteristics, but also at the powers with which it was endowed.

In the specific case of parliaments and parliamentary oversight, Pelizzo and Stapenhurst (2006) suggested that our understanding of whether and to what extent parliaments are able to effectively perform their oversight function would increase if more attention was paid to the number and the type of oversight tools that parliaments can employ to perform their oversight tasks.

If we look at these characteristics, we find that there are some detectable differences between the legislature in Nigeria and in Ghana. While both legislatures have parliamentary PACs, motions of censure, and the power to impeach the president, both lack the tool of a vote of no confidence, and only in Ghana is there question time. Furthermore, Ghana and Nigeria have similar webs of extra-legislative oversight tools—they both have Auditors General, ombuds offices, and anti-corruption agencies, although they differ in terms of the staff support and library facilities. Respondents reported that library facilities and staff support is very poor in Ghana, but somewhat better in Nigeria.

In Tables 4.1 and 4.2, we present basic information concerning Ghana and Nigeria. Table 4.1 shows that, with regard to five of the 10 macro-level characteristics, there is no difference between the two countries and only minor differences with regard to an additional two. There is a major difference in three respects, namely the size of the country, the form of state, and the strength of political parties. We examine these three factors in greater detail.

It has long been established that there is a strong, positive, and significant relationship between wealth and corruption, which is one of the indicators of development and good governance. In other words, countries that are richer are less corrupt. The data presented in Table 4.1 show that while both countries are low-income countries, the GDP per capita is 40 percent higher in Nigeria than in Ghana and, therefore, should be associated with, and possibly conducive to, less corruption.[2]

Several studies, including those undertaken by the World Bank (Mody, 2004), have pointed out that the size of the country may represent an administrative challenge; create the conditions for inefficiency, ineffectiveness, and arbitrary behavior; and, worst of all, could create the proper conditions for misallocation of resources and corruption. Devolution is one of the solutions that has been advocated or invoked to solve the problem. The idea,

Table 4.1 The Context—Ghana and Nigeria in Comparative Perspective

	GHANA	NIGERIA	
Region	West Africa	West Africa	No difference
Size of country	Small	Big	Major difference
Population	Ethnically fragmented	Ethnically fragmented	No difference
British colonial legacy	Yes	Yes	No difference
Stable constitutional order after independence	No	No	No difference
Presidential form of government	Partial	Yes	Minor difference
Electoral system	FPTP	FPTP	No difference
Form of state	Unitary	Federal	Major difference
GDP per capita (US $)	1,000	1,400	Minor difference
Political parties	Two, very strong	Several, relatively weak	Major difference

simply put, is that if and when services are brought closer to the citizens, it is easier for citizens to assess the quality of the products and services, act as watchdogs, voice discontent, denounce inefficiencies or ineffectiveness of services and programs, and, by doing so, minimize the instances of corruption. If this is indeed the case, Ghana, should be less corrupt because of size, but Nigeria could be less corrupt because it has a federal instead of a unitary form of state. Hence, in terms of the broad, general context, Nigeria holds a small edge over Ghana.

With regard to the strength of political parties, it is not entirely clear whether and to what extent party strength may affect a parliament's ability to effectively perform its oversight function and the level of corruption. The confusion in this regard is due to two factors. The first is the notion of party strength. This notion has been used by political scientists to denote the share of the vote a party is able to win, the share of the seats a party controls in a legislature, its financial resources, its institutionalization, or the level of discipline or cohesion that its members display. In other words, party strength may be measured in votes, seats, income, age, and party cohesion—characteristics that may or may not go together. Political scientists, from Sartori (1976) onward, have described African party systems as fluid because they are characterized by the presence of short-lived dominant parties that win overwhelming majorities of the vote—hence age of a political party and success at the ballot box may not be two sides of the same coin. Furthermore, there are contradictory claims as to whether party cohesion is beneficial to the effectiveness of oversight activity. For instance, several studies on oversight (Rockman, 1984; Beetham, 2006) suggested that a high level of partisanship (which occurs when sizeable majorities of two or more parties oppose one another on a majority of issues) is beneficial to oversight because when the opposition parties are mobilized against the ruling party, both they and parliament are more likely to effectively perform their watchdog and oversight functions. In short, partisanship is believed to be a necessary prerequisite for effective oversight. This line of thinking holds the view that government members will never take seriously their oversight tasks because their primary interest is to protect their government. Thus, effective oversight will occur only if the opposition forces are mobilized against the government, if only with the hope of scoring some political points. But this view neglects the fact that parliamentarians have an institutional as well as a partisan affiliation; in addition to having loyalty to their party, they also have loyalty to the institution of parliament.[3]

Going back to our comparison, it is difficult to say whether—as far as political parties are concerned—the parliament of Ghana may outperform the legislature in Nigeria in the exercise of oversight. Not only is it unclear whether and how political party strength should affect oversight performance, but also our field research shows an interesting phenomenon: While the parties in Ghana are stronger than their Nigerian counterparts, the responses from our survey respondents and focus group members revealed that Nigerian parliamentarians are more partisan in their behavior than their Ghanaian counterparts! While there are clear differences in terms of the structure, format, and mechanics of the political party system and in the level of party cohesion and partisanship, the field results do not provide a clear indication of which legislature should be a more effective overseer and thus be better equipped to curb corruption.

The evidence presented in Tables 4.1 and 4.2 sustains the claim that there is little difference between the case of Nigeria and that of Ghana in terms of oversight capacity.

Table 4.2 Oversight Capacity—Oversight Tools and Facilitating Conditions

	Nigerian National Assembly (NASS)	Ghanaian Parliament
Oversight tools		
Audit committees	2 x Public Accounts Committees	Public Accounts Committee
Other committees	Strong; well resourced	Tend to be weak; poorly resourced
Question period	No	Yes
Cabinet formation/ dismissal	Ministers (who cannot be members of NASS) selected by president; ratified by NASS	Selected by president; 60% must be MPs; ratified by parliament
Censure/impeach	NASS can censure ministers and impeach the president	Parliament can censure ministers and impeach the president

(Continued)

Table 4.2   (Continued)

	Nigerian National Assembly (NASS)	Ghanaian Parliament
Vote of no confidence	NASS cannot shorten president's fixed term of office, except through impeachment	No
Supreme audit institution	Audit office	Audit office
Ombuds office	Prevention of Corruption Commission	Commission on Human Rights and Administrative Justice
Anti-corruption agencies	Independent Corrupt Practices & Related Offences Commission; Economic & Financial Crimes Commission	Serious Fraud Office
Facilitating conditions		
Staff + research facilities	Somewhat poor	Very poor
Access to information law	No	No

OVERSIGHT ACTIVITY AND THE ROLE OF PARLIAMENT IN CURBING CORRUPTION

When we switch the focus of our attention from the oversight tools at the disposal of the legislature to the oversight activities performed, we find that the Nigerian legislature is slightly more active than the Ghanaian parliament in reviewing appointments and censuring ministers, but is slightly less active with regard to the number of committee meetings held in the course of the legislative session, while there is no real difference in terms of attendance of plenary meetings. (See Table 4.3.)

The general context, considered previously, the oversight capacity, the number of oversight tools at the disposal of the legislature, and the amount of activities performed, presented above, would lead one to expect that the Nigerian legislature is substantially more effective than the Ghanaian parliament. The field data presented in Tables 4.3 and 4.4 are consistent with this expectation. The data presented in Table 4.4 reveal that special parliamentary committees are believed to be equally effective in Ghana and Nigeria in uncovering incidents of corruption, while oversight committees are believed to be slightly more effective in Nigeria than in Ghana.

Yet, in spite of the fact that the Nigerian and the Ghanaian legislatures are (or, at least, are believed to be) equally effective in performing their oversight tasks and detecting corruption, the level of perceived corruption in the

Table 4.3   Internal Tools and Mechanisms Influencing Legislative Oversight

Survey Question	Ghana		Nigeria	
	Mean score	Std. dev.	Mean score	Std. dev.
How frequently does the legislature review appointments?	3.5	1.7	4.6	1.0
How frequently does the legislature censure ministers/the president?	1.7	0.8	2.1	0.9
What is the degree of partisanship within legislative oversight committees?	2.2	1.6	2.8	1.3
How often do oversight committees meet during a legislative session?	10 times	9 times	4.3	1.1
What percentage of legislators attend plenary sessions?	65%	0.8	67%	0.8

Scale of 1–5, where 1 = very weak/never and 5 = very effective/always

Table 4.4   Legislative Effectiveness in Curbing Corruption

	Ghana		Nigeria	
	Mean score	Std. dev.	Mean score	Std. dev.
How effective are oversight committees in uncovering incidents of fraud and corruption?	3.2	1.5	3.5	1.1
How effective are special committees/ commissions of inquiry in uncovering incidents of fraud and corruption?	3.8	1.3	3.9	1.1

Scale of 1–5, where 1 = very weak/never and 5 = very effective/always

two countries is substantially different. In 2013, Ghana had a CPI score of 4.5, while Nigeria received a CPI score of only 2.7; Ghana ranks 64th in the world in terms of corruption, while Nigeria ranks 139th. Furthermore, 67 percent of Ghanaian respondents believe their parliament to be somewhat or extremely corrupt, while 79 percent of Nigerian respondents believe their legislature to be corrupt. (See Table 4.5.)

Results are presented in Table 4.6. Three results are worth mentioning. First, in both Ghana and Nigeria, the percentage of respondents who believed legislators to be involved in corruption exceeded the percentage of

Table 4.5   Corruption in Ghana and Nigeria

	Ghana	Nigeria
Corruption perception index	4.5	2.7
Corruption perception index—ranking	64th	139th
Percentage of respondents who believe parliament to be corrupt or extremely corrupt	67	79

Source: The data on CPI are taken from Transparency International; the information on the percentage of respondents believing parliament to be corrupt are taken from Transparency International's Corruption Barometer (2013).

Table 4.6   How Many of the Following People Do You Think Are Involved in Corruption? Percentage of respondents; n = 1,200 (Ghana) and n = 2,324 (Nigeria)

	Ghana			Nigeria		
	Most/all	Some	Total	Most/all	Some	Total
President and officials in his office	17	53	70	37	51	88
Legislators	19	54	73	51	38	89
Local government councilors	19	52	71	55	37	92
Government officials	27	51	78	56	36	92
Police	22	74	76	71	22	93
Tax officials	32	47	79	53	35	88
Judges and magistrates	29	50	79	36	49	75

Source: Afrobarometer 2008 survey; available online at www.afrobarometer.org. Afrobarometer is an independent, nonpartisan research project that measures the social, political, and economic atmosphere in Africa. They asked respondents to indicate which "people"—that is politicians and other public figures—are believed to be involved in corrupt activities.

respondents who believed the executive to be corrupt. Second, the percentage of respondents who reported that either "most/all" or "some" legislators are involved in corruption was much higher in Nigeria (89 percent) than in Ghana (73 percent)—a result that was magnified by the fact that a simple majority of respondents suggested that "all/most" legislators in Nigeria are corrupt. Third, if we add the percentage of respondents who believe "most/all" and "some" people to be corrupt, we find that of the seven categories of public officials, legislators are the third least corrupt public officials in Ghana and the fourth least corrupt in Nigeria.

Nigerian MPs are perceived to be more corrupt than their colleagues in Ghana. But Nigerian judges, tax officials, policemen, government officials, and local councilors, are all perceived to be dramatically more corrupt than their Ghanaian counterparts.

Regardless of whether Nigeria is objectively more corrupt and whether respondents have a systemic bias that leads them to believe that corruption is objectively more widespread in one country than in the other, the perception of widespread corruption in Nigeria and the perception of a corrupt parliament and legislators in both countries has far-reaching consequences.

CORRUPTION AND LEGITIMACY

The most significant consequence of perceived legislative corruption is that it affects the level of legitimacy of the legislative branch of government. Table 4.7 shows that 62 percent of the Ghanaian respondents have some trust in their parliament, while only 33 percent of Nigerian respondents have some trust in their legislature. In addition to all the problems we have documented in Chapter 2—that corruption results to lower economic growth, higher infant mortality, lower rates of adult literacy, and so on—corruption also erodes the legitimacy of institutions. Worse, perhaps, is that the mere perception of corruption erodes the legitimacy of an institution: In spite of the fact that even though in several respects the Nigerian legislature is considerably more active as an overseer than its Ghanaian equivalent, Nigerians have less trust in it.

The level of legitimacy of an institution is directly related to its perceived integrity: Corrupt institutions suffer low levels of legitimacy, while transparent institutions enjoy high levels of legitimacy.

While there is no objective empirical evidence to sustain the claim that Nigerian legislators are indeed more corrupt than their Ghanaian counterparts, there is little doubt that respondents in surveys such as the ones

Table 4.7 How Much Trust Do You Have in the Following Institutions?

	Ghana			Nigeria		
	A lot	Some-what	Total	A lot	Some-what	Total
President	56	19	75	15	30	45
Parliament/National Assembly	35	27	72	7	26	33
Electoral Commission	40	36	86	6	22	38
Local Government Council	28	25	63	6	22	28
Ruling Party	42	24	67	7	22	29
Opposition Party	22	26	48	7	22	29
Police	28	18	46	8	17	23
Courts of Law	30	28	58	10	30	40
Traditional Leaders	41	25	66	15	30	45

Percentage of respondents; n = 1,200 (Ghana) and n = 2,324 (Nigeria)
Source: Afrobarometer 2008 survey; available online at www.afrobarometer.org.

conducted by Afrobarometer believe that they are. Why is this? We believe that there are two very simple reasons why the Nigerian legislature is believed to be more corrupt than the parliament of Ghana. The first is reputation. Nigeria as a country is believed to be more corrupt than Ghana, and each and every institution or group of public officials in Nigeria is believed to be more corrupt than those in Ghana; hence, regardless of its real level of corruption, the Nigerian legislature is perceived to be more corrupt because it operates in a more corrupt context. A second reason is that, in spite of its activism, its activities, is powers, its resources, and its performance, the level of perceived corruption in Nigeria remains fairly high. The fact that the actions of the Nigerian legislature seem to have no impact on the overall level of corruption may be taken as an unequivocal sign of its ineffectiveness. And since this ineffectiveness is combined with a very low level of legitimacy, it is easy for the cynical observer to draw the conclusion that the reason why the Nigerian legislature fails to significantly curb corruption in the country is that it has no interest in doing so, because it is a corrupt institution and does not want to destroy the system of corruption from which its members benefit.

However, the evidence at our disposal suggests a different conclusion. The reason why the Nigerian legislature is not terribly effective in curbing corruption is due to a simple reason: The contextual factors that should help the Nigerian legislature to perform its oversight task are quite ineffective and are remarkably less effective than their Ghanaian counterparts. Hence, the Nigerian legislature's struggles to curb corruption do not stem from its inability or unwillingness to fight and eradicate corruption, but are due to the fact that it may not receive adequate support from the supreme audit institution, the anti-corruption agencies, and the ombudsperson. These institutions have not been as effective as their counterparts in Ghana in fighting corruption, as can be seen in Table 4.8.

The implication of this is that the Nigerian legislature shares the blame for the failure of other public institutions in doing their job. But the fact that

Table 4.8 External Tools and Mechanisms Influencing Legislative Oversight

Survey question	Ghana		Nigeria	
	Mean score	Std. dev.	Mean score	Std. dev.
How effective is the Auditor General in uncovering incidents of fraud and corruption?	4.2	0.9	2.6	1.2
How effective is the Ombudsman in uncovering incidents of fraud and corruption?	3.6	0.8	2.8	1.7
How effective is the Anti-Corruption Agency in uncovering incidents of fraud and corruption?	3.5	1.3	3.3	1.1

Scale of 1–5, where 1 = very weak and 5 = very effective

it suffers such a low level of trust and legitimacy means that the legislature cannot count on widespread popular support in performing its tasks, which further undermines its ability to tackle corruption.

This comparative analysis teaches a very simple lesson, namely that no matter how important legislatures are in the institutional architecture of democratic regimes, no matter how important the functions are that legislatures perform, and no matter how important legislative oversight is for curbing corruption, it is necessary to take a more comprehensive, holistic approach. Specifically, in addition to ensuring that legislatures are both equipped and willing—a theme that we will discuss at greater length later on in this book—to perform their oversight function and to fight corruption, it is also necessary to take steps to ensure that legislatures behave in an honest, transparent, and ethical manner and that they enjoy the confidence and the trust of their citizens.

CONCLUSIONS

The purpose of this chapter was straightforward. We presented an in-depth comparative analysis to show that in countries with broadly comparable characteristics in terms of geographic location, colonial legacy, institutional history, socio-economic development, electoral system, and ethnic composition of society, there may be major differences in both the level of corruption and in a legislature's ability to curb corruption. We further noted that, a priori, the conditions for more effective oversight—and thus more successful anti-corruption efforts—existed in Nigeria. But in fact, Ghana is perceived to be less corrupt than Nigeria, and the Ghanaian parliament is believed to be more effective than the Nigerian legislature in helping curb corruption.

We went on to show that this variation in effectiveness is due to the external oversight tools and contextual factors that influence and support the legislature in performing its oversight tasks. The Nigerian legislature is blamed for the poor performance of the institutions that should support it in the fight against corruption, and it thus loses legitimacy in the eyes of the population. This loss of legitimacy is detrimental not only because it undermines popular support for the constitutional order, the existing political system, and the current political institutional arrangements, but also because it undermines the performance of the legislature itself. Popular support for a legislature is essential for ensuring that the legislature itself is effective in performing its oversight task (Pelizzo and Stapenhurst, 2012).

This is why we suggested that while the ability of legislatures to oversee the executive and the expenditure of public money and government accounts should be strengthened, it is also important to take other, non-legislative measures: It should be ensured that the institutions that support the legislature to do their job effectively, that the legislature be made as corruption-free as possible, and that steps be taken to enable the legislature to regain citizen trust. Without these, a legislature cannot work well.

NOTES

1. In 2008–9, we interviewed some 50 legislators, parliamentary staff, journalists, and civil society representatives in both Ghana and Nigeria. In both countries, we used a common survey instrument and conducted four focus groups, each of which comprised between four and seven participants, to complement data obtained through interviews. A fifth focus group was conducted with a selection of earlier (interview) participants, and preliminary analyses and conclusions were presented and validated. See Stapenhurst (2011).
2. In Chapter 2, we discussed extensively why individual wealth and development, or rather the lack thereof, provide corruption with fertile ground in which to flourish.
3. The loyalty that legislators have for the institution is quite clear in the case of PACs, whose success have been credited, above all, to parliamentarians' ability to work in a non-partisan fashion (McGee, 2002; Stapenhurst et al, 2005; Stapenhurst, Pelizzo, and Jacobs, 2013).

REFERENCES

Beetham, D. (2006). *Parliament and Democracy in the Twenty-first Century.* Geneva: IPU.

McGee, D. (2002). *The Overseers.* London: Pluto Press.

Mody, J. (2004). Achieving Accountability through Decentralization: Lessons for Integrated River Basin Management. *World Bank Policy Research Working Paper,* 3346.

Pelizzo, R., and R. Stapenhurst. (2006). "Democracy and Oversight." Paper presented at the 102nd Annual Meeting of the American Political Science Association, Philadelphia, August 31–September 3.

Pelizzo, R., and R. Stapenhurst. (2012). *Parliamentary Oversight Tools.* London: Routledge.

Pelizzo, R., and R. Stapenhurst. (2013). *Government Accountability and Legislative Oversight.* New York: Routledge.

Rockman, B. A. (1984). Legislative—Executive Relations and Legislative Oversight. *Legislative Studies Quarterly,* 9(3), 387–440.

Sartori, G. (1976). *Parties and Party Systems.* New York: Cambridge University Press.

Stapenhurst, R., R. Pelizzo, and K. Jacobs (2013). *Following the Money: Comparing Parliamentary Public Accounts Committees.* London: Pluto Press.

Stapenhurst, R., V. Bahgal, W. Woodley, and R. Pelizzo. (2005). "Scrutinizing Public Expenditures: Assessing the Performance of PACS." *World Bank Research Paper* No. 3613. May 2005.

5 Legislative Corruption, Public Trust, and Political Will

INTRODUCTION

As noted in Chapters 1 and 3, Jain (2002, p. 75) highlighted the issue of legislative corruption, defining it as: ". . . the manner and the extent to which the voting behavior of legislators can be influenced. Legislators can be bribed by interest groups to enact legislation that [favors their clients/members]. This type of corruption . . . include[s] vote-buying, whether by legislators in their attempts to get re-elected or by officials in the executive branch in their efforts to have some legislation enacted."

International organizations and practitioners have long believed that legislatures are the agents of society, that they enjoy the confidence of the public, that they are relatively free from corruption and other types of illegal behavior, and that they can play a key role in promoting reduced corruption since they are constitutionally mandated to oversee the executive and keep it accountable. While it is unconditionally true that parliaments and legislatures are representative bodies and have both a constitutional and popular mandate to oversee the executive, some of these assumptions are only conditionally true or, worse, entirely out of touch with the real world.

A succession of scandals uncovered in recent years have it made clear that legislatures are not free of corruption, that some legislatures are indeed quite involved in corrupt or illicit activities, and that many of those legislatures or legislators that do not engage in any illicit, illegal, criminal activity, are often involved in unethical forms of behavior such as, for example, conflicts of interests.

Furthermore, there is considerable evidence not only of the fact that legislatures are not free of corruption, but also that they do not always enjoy the confidence of their own citizens. In this chapter, we present some evidence of this, propose some manifestations of legislative malfeasance, and propose a dynamic model that explains such behavior.

PUBLIC TRUST IN LEGISLATURES

For the past 32 years, the World Value Survey has conducted worldwide surveys to collect information on political culture, social and cultural values, and the like.[1] One set of questions included in its survey concerns the confidence that citizens have in a variety of organizations, such as the Church, the armed forces, the education system, the press, labor unions, the police, parliament, civil service, television, the government, and political parties. The analysis of these data has regularly revealed two facts: The first is that legislatures enjoy very little public confidence relative to that enjoyed by other institutions; the second is that legislatures also enjoy very little confidence in absolute terms. In other words, it is not simply that the citizens have less confidence in parliament than in other institutions, but that citizens rank legislative institutions among the lowest of institutions with public trust.

Respondents worldwide were asked to indicate whether they had "a great deal," "quite a lot," "not so much," or "no" confidence in various institutions—including parliament. The results of analysis of the data collected in the fourth wave (2005–2008) of the World Value Survey are presented in Table 5.1.

As can be seen from Table 5.1, the data were collected from among 53 countries and display considerable variation. For instance the percentage of respondents indicating to have "a great deal" of confidence in parliament varies from a minimum of 0.9 percent in Serbia to a maximum of 78.4 percent in Vietnam, with an average of 9.3 percent. And, of course the percentage would be considerably lower if Vietnam (an outlier) was removed from statistical consideration.[2] The percentage of respondents indicating to have "quite a lot" of confidence in parliament varies from a minimum of 5.4 percent in Peru to 52.5 percent in China, with an average of 29.3 percent.

If we combine the percentage of respondents reporting to have "a great deal" of confidence with those reporting to have "quite a lot of confidence" in parliament, the result provides an indication of the confidence enjoyed by national legislatures in their respective countries. The data on the total amount of confidence that legislatures enjoy worldwide are presented in the third column of Table 5.1. The data show that this confidence varies from a minimum of 7.8 percent in Peru to a maximum of 98.8 percent in Vietnam, with an average of 38.9 percent. Again, if we treat Vietnam as an outlier and remove it from consideration, confidence in parliament varies from the minimum recorded in Peru to a maximum of 92.4 percent registered in China. It is somewhat ironic that the data show that in highly democratic settings parliaments are not held in particularly high esteem by their citizens, while in countries that are not known for the quality of their democracy (China, Vietnam) or that have experienced what some might call "state failure" (such as Mali and Rwanda), parliaments enjoy considerably higher amounts of confidence.

The conclusion to be drawn is clear. Most citizens around the world have very little trust in parliament, such confidence in parliament is particularly

Table 5.1   Confidence in Parliament (Percentage of Respondents)

	"A great deal"	"Quite a lot"	Total
Vietnam	78.4	20.4	98.8
China	39.9	52.5	92.4
Rwanda	31.5	47.3	78.8
Mali	21.8	35.2	77
Malaysia	18.5	49	67.5
South Africa	24.6	41	65.6
Ghana	22.2	42.7	64.9
Jordan	34.6	30	64.6
India	27.4	35	62.4
Norway	5.2	57.1	62.3
Turkey	22.7	38.8	61.5
Sweden	4.4	51.9	56.3
Finland	4.9	51.2	56.1
Switzerland	3.1	50.9	54
Hong Kong	2.8	48.7	51.5
Spain	5.7	45.1	50.8
Cyprus	12.6	36.4	49
Uruguay	7.4	40	47.4
Morocco	14.2	30.3	44.5
Iran	12.8	28.7	41.5
Burkina Faso	9.6	29.1	38.7
Canada	3.8	34.4	38.2
Indonesia	4.5	32.2	36.7
Great Britain	4.9	31.3	36.2
France	2.9	32.6	35.5
New Zealand	3.2	31.4	34.6
Australia	4.2	29.9	34.1
Italy	1.7	31.3	33
Thailand	5	27.7	32.7
Russia	2.4	27.5	29.9
Netherlands	1	28.7	29.7
Moldova	5.5	22.5	28
South Korea	1.4	24.8	26.2
Mexico	3.7	21.7	25.4
Colombia	3.6	21.8	25.4
Brazil	2.7	22.2	24.9
Georgia	3.2	21.7	24.9
Chile	3	21.5	24.5

(Continued)

Table 5.1 (Continued)

	"A great deal"	"Quite a lot"	Total
Ethiopia	5.6	18.5	24.1
Japan	1.2	22	23.2
Germany	1.2	20.7	21.9
Bulgaria	3.8	17.1	20.9
USA	1.5	19.1	20.6
Serbia	0.9	19.7	20.6
Ukraine	2.9	16.9	19.8
Romania	1.4	15.7	17.1
Slovenia	1.7	14.7	16.4
Trinidad & Tobago	2.7	13.5	16.2
Taiwan	1.5	12.6	14.1
Argentina	0.9	12.7	13.6
Poland	1.4	10.8	12.2
Guatemala	1.9	9.5	11.4
Peru	2.4	5.4	7.8

Source: World Value Survey 2005–2008

low in highly advanced industrial economies (Japan), in established democracies (the United States), and in Latin American and Eastern European countries. We return to this issue and strategies that legislatures are adopting to reverse this situation in Chapter 6.

PUBLIC TRUST IN PARLIAMENTS AND LEGISLATIVE CORRUPTION

Not only do citizens have little trust in parliaments, but parliaments are regarded among the most corrupt institutions. Transparency International every year collects and presents several datasets on corruption. The most common dataset provides an indication of how much corruption is perceived to exist in some countries. Of interest to us, however, is the Corruption Barometer, which provides, inter alia, an indication of the level of corruption within various institutions.

The data presented in the latest Global Corruption Barometer (involving 11 institutions in 100 countries) show that parliaments are regarded as the most corrupt public institutions in a number of countries (Brazil, Colombia, Indonesia, Korea, Lithuania, Maldives, Mongolia, Romania, Solomon Islands, and Tanzania) and that globally, parliaments are considered the second most corrupt institutions, after political parties. For details, see Figure 5.1.

What is remarkable is that there seems to be a very high correspondence between the percentage of respondents who have little to no trust in parliament

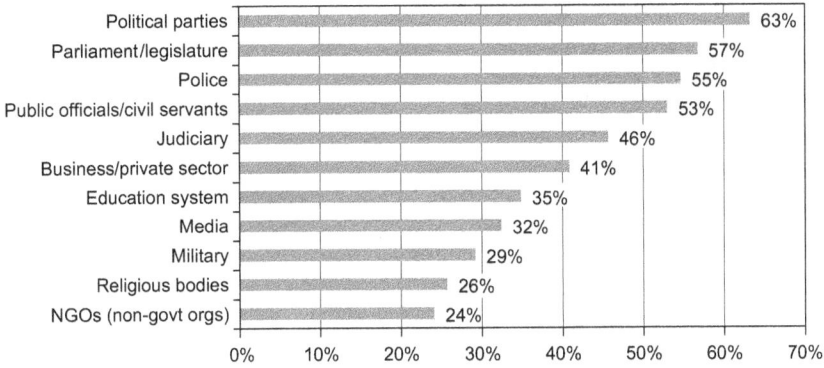

Figure 5.1   Percentage of Respondents Viewing Public Institutions as Corrupt (n = 100)
Source: Transparency International, Corruption Barometer

and those who think that parliaments are corrupt.[3] To check whether there is indeed a relationship between corruption of parliaments and the amount of confidence that citizens have in parliament, we correlate the percentage of voters who report having confidence in parliament with the percentage of respondents who believe parliament to be corrupt (see Figure 5.2).

Using correlation analysis, it emerges that there is a strong, negative, and significant relationship between corruption and confidence: the higher the percentage of voters believing that parliament is corrupt, the lower the confidence, and vice versa—as we can see in Figure 5.2. The correlation between these two variables is fairly strong ($r = -.478$, sig. 001). But we believe that what appears at first as a simple association or correlation between these two variables could in reality be understood as a causal relationship. In other words, it is not by accident that where people think that the parliament is corrupt, they have little trust in parliament. We believe that it is precisely because voters think that parliament is corrupt that they have very little trust in parliament. By assuming that the perception of corruption is responsible for the low levels of trust, we can integrate our correlation analysis with a simple regression analysis.[4] By doing so we are able to generate information in two respects. First, how much does a change in the percentage of voters believing that parliament is corrupt affect the percentage of voters having confidence in parliament? Second, what portion of the variance in the percentage of voters having no confidence in parliament is explained by changes in the percentage of voters who believe that parliament is corrupt?

The basic regression model that we will use in the course of the present analysis is

$$y = a + b1X1 + e$$

where y is the percentage of voters who have confidence in parliament, X is the percentage of voters who think that parliament is corrupt, and b is the amount of change in y which is caused by a one-unit increase in X.

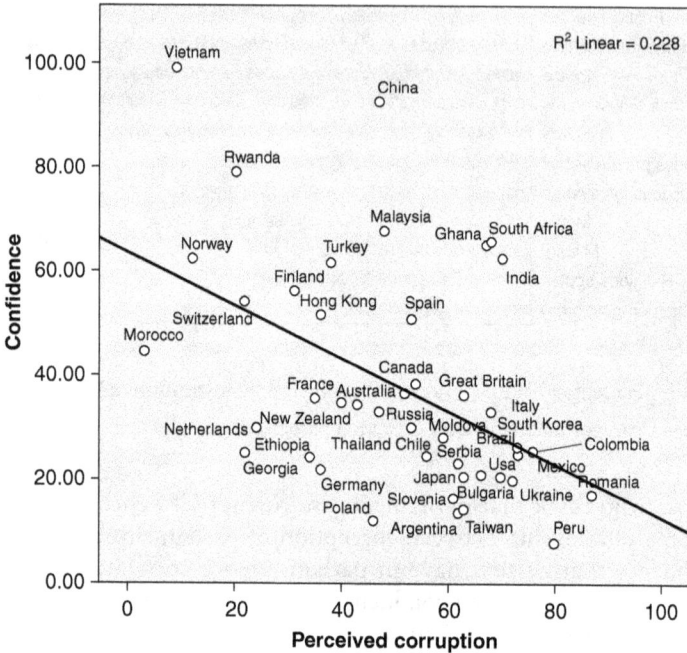

Figure 5.2   Perceived Corruption and Confidence in Parliament

By running this regression we find that the regression takes the following value:

$$y = 63.43 - .503X$$

This means a 1 percent increase in the percentage of voters who believe parliament is corrupt leads to a .5 decrease in the percentage of voters who have confidence in parliament, that a 10 percent increase in the percentage of those who perceive corruption leads to a 5 percent loss in the percentage of voters that have confidence in parliament, and so on.

With regard to the second question, the evidence generated by our regression model suggests that the percentage of voters believing parliament to be corrupt accounts by itself for about 23 percent of the variance in the percentage of voters who have confidence in parliament (R-squared = .228).

As we saw in Chapter 2, corruption is detrimental because misallocating resources, creating a distorted system of incentives, and increasing the transactions costs discourages investors, undermines growth, and represents a major obstacle for development.

Corruption poses additional threats to the proper functioning of a political system: It erodes the representativeness and the legitimacy of the political institutions.

In democratic settings, the representativeness of the elected bodies, of elected officials, and of the political system are ensured by the fact that some minimal conditions are respected: there is universal suffrage (people have the right to vote—active electorate); people have the right to run for office if they so wish (people have the right to run in the elections and be voted—passive electorate); they have the right to make their ideas, opinions, proposals, and programs known to the electorate; and they should be elected to office by the electorate on the basis of the quality of their programmatic proposals. Representative or democratic elections are the most noticeable embodiment of the principle of equality that characterizes democratic systems because in democratic elections, every individual has the right to cast a ballot, and any ballot or vote is as important as any other.

Corruption violates these conditions. Candidates who raise money illicitly by accepting bribes, kickbacks, and other illegal campaign contributions are able to outspend their competitors, get more visibility, and in complete violation of the law, buy votes. Corruption alters the playing field on which candidates compete against one another and may set the stage for other violations of the law.

Corruption also violates the principle of equality because the individuals who pay bribes to politicians and provide illicit contributions to party finance develop special relationships with the politicians and can use these relationships to manipulate the political system for private gain.

Corruption hence leads to the under-representativeness of elected officials, legislative assemblies, and the political system and to the adoption and implementation of sub-optimal socio-economic policies. This under-representativeness and these sub-optimal policies are largely responsible for the fact that large and increasing segments of the electorates have little to no confidence in legislators, legislatures, and political systems.

Political scientists from Lipset (1959) onward have long held the view that confidence in the political system—what political scientists call "legitimacy"—is the single most important condition for the survival, the duration, and the preservation of a political system (democratic or otherwise).

Legitimacy can be derived from a variety of sources: from the charisma of a political leader, from the ideology of the ruling party (in totalitarian regimes), from rules and procedures (in democratic settings), and from performance (in all systems). Performance-based legitimacy is particularly important for authoritarian regimes, which lack the kind of legitimacy that totalitarian and democratic regimes derive respectively from ideology and elections. But performance-based legitimacy is important for all political regimes because if a regime is unable to deliver to the needs of the citizens, it will lose its legitimacy and it will be replaced by some other political system.

By inducing legislatures, governments, and political systems to pursue and implement sub-optimal policies and by reducing the representativeness of democratic institutions and systems, corruption can be responsible for the loss of legitimacy and for a system breakdown.

POLITICAL WILL

For the past 15 years or so, international organizations, scholars, and practitioners have believed in a set of intertwined assumptions, namely that corruption was detrimental for economic growth and development, that corruption could be curbed by creating systems of accountability, that effective oversight is instrumental in setting up such systems of accountability, and that oversight effectiveness is a quasi-automatic consequence of the powers placed in the hands of the overseers. If the overseers have wide powers, wide mandates, and a wide range of oversight tools at their disposal, they will be very effective in the performance of their oversight function.

While this view has been fairly influential and has provided practitioners with some guidance, recent studies have questioned the validity of some of these assumptions. The work by Pelizzo and Stapenhurst (2012) has shown that corruption affects development and that effective oversight plays a key role in curbing corruption, but they have also shown that there is no relationship between the number of oversight tools at the disposal of a legislature and the effectiveness with which it performs its oversight function.

Pelizzo and Stapenhurst (2012) and Stapenhurst, Pelizzo, and Jacobs (2013) later on have suggested that oversight capacity (number of tools and powers) translates into effective oversight on one condition: that the overseers have the political will to use the power and the tools at their disposal to keep governments accountable for their action, for their expenditures, and for their policy implementation and execution.

These studies underlined that political will—the will to make effective use of the oversight tools—is the single most important determinant of effective oversight. However, it is not the only cause. The effectiveness in the performance of the oversight function is also affected by the number and the types of tools at the disposal of a legislature; by the amount of human, technical, and financial resources placed at disposal of the overseers; and by the context in which the overseers operate. But none of these factors is as important as political will.

While most of the previous studies have underlined the importance of political will in ensuring that oversight is performed effectively and the executives are held accountable and how effective oversight and accountability play a key role in curbing corruption, little attention has been paid to the other side of the equation, namely to the impact that corruption has on the political will of the overseers.

The impact of corruption on the political will to promote good governance is always detrimental, regardless of whether corruption is real or just perceived, objective or subjective. We need to discuss each of these two scenarios separately.

If a legislature is perceived to be corrupt, regardless of whether it is actually corrupt, it enjoys very little popular support, little confidence and trust. This lack of trust has a negative impact on a legislature's ability to be an effective overseer. If the legislature has no popular backing, it may not have either the strength or the will to oversee the executive effectively. It can more easily be blamed for the ineffective implementation of government policy—(the government policy was good, but the legislature watered it down; the government policy was good, but the legislature did not allow us to implement it; the government policy was good, but we could not act more swiftly because the legislature slowed us down; and so on). The comparative evidence has consistently shown that unless there is overwhelming evidence against the executive, the people are more likely to support the executive than the legislature. The comparative evidence has also shown that whenever there is an inter-institutional struggle, the outcome is usually that the approval rate of the executive increases and that of the legislature decreases. Hence, if a legislature has little trust to begin with, engaging in effective oversight may lead to dangerously low levels of trust and approval and have devastating electoral consequences.

If a legislature is corrupt, it has no incentive to change the system from which it benefits—which is the reason why legislative oversight, however important, cannot possibly be the only instrument to fight corruption.

Hence to ensure that legislatures are effective overseers and in order to secure that legislatures effectively perform their oversight function, they need to enjoy some public trust and be relatively free from corruption, as we will discuss at greater length in the next few chapters

REGAINING PUBLIC TRUST

In order to regain the confidence of the citizens, parliaments have taken several steps: They have adopted Codes of Ethics and Codes of Conduct, they have introduced dispositions concerning the disclosure and the registration of interests, and they have in several cases set up ethics committees in parliament. Such regimes are adopted in response to legitimacy crises. In Chapter 6, we highlight the differences between these two types of codes, paying particular attention to the fact that Codes of Conduct are more detailed, are not aspirational, and establish clear sanctions for violations of the norms they set for parliamentarians. But while these dispositions regulate the behavior of members after they are elected and are meant to prevent instances of corrupt and unethical behavior in parliament, they do very little in preventing the election of corrupt candidates or in preventing/minimizing/eradicating electoral corruption.

As we will see in Chapter 7, several normative and legal dispositions have been introduced to curb electoral corruption. Since it is generally believed that the single most important determinant of electoral corruption is the cost of campaigning, some dispositions have been introduced to place limits on how much money parties and candidates may spend in the course of an election and instead to provide parties and candidates with public subsidies and free/cheap broadcasting. In other instances, limits have been placed on the amounts of private and corporate funds that parties and candidates are allowed to accept. Campaign regulations have been introduced in various jurisdictions involving strict norms, monitoring bodies, and sanctions for violations.

In Chapter 7 we also consider campaign finance regulations. We make clear that in the course of the past two decades, partially in response to various corruption scandals, several campaign finance regulations have been introduced to eliminate electoral and campaign corruption. We will show that campaign finance regulations cover four distinct areas: Some of these dispositions place bans and limitations on the sources and the amounts of funds that parties and candidates can receive; some dispositions concern public funding, financial subsidies and subsidies in kind, to both political parties and electoral candidates; some dispositions are intended to regulate the level of spending; while a fourth set of dispositions concerns the report mechanisms and the oversight of campaign finance as well as the sanctions that can be applied for violations of campaign legislation.

The example of Anti-Money Laundering legislation and to how it can beneficial in detecting political corruption is presented in the Expert Monograph, at the end of this book.

LEGISLATIVE NETWORKS TO COMBAT CORRUPTION

In 1998, at a seminar organized by the World Bank Institute and the Parliamentary Centre[5] and hosted by the Parliament of Uganda, the African Parliamentarians Network Against Corruption (APNAC) was founded. APNAC focuses on coordinating, involving, and strengthening the capacity of African parliamentarians to fight corruption and is the model on which the Global Organization of Parliamentarians Against Corruption (GOPAC)[6] was founded, some three years later.

Such networks promote the political will of parliamentarians to combat corruption by showing why curbing corruption is an essential component of any poverty-reduction and development-promotion strategy. Such networks have also provided information and knowledge. Networks conducted (or commissioned scholars and practitioners to conduct) applied research into what parliaments can do to curb corruption, to create the conditions for sustainable growth, and to reduce poverty. Parliamentarians who could not find support for combating corruption within their own countries were able to find support among peers in other countries through these networks. This strengthened the global coalition against corruption and established peer support networks where parliamentarians could learn from the efforts of their colleagues. Attention was paid to studying the institutional devices that parliaments can employ to oversee the activities and the expenditures of the executive and to control the behavior of legislators and of the legislature as a whole.

Several publications have been produced on the basis of such research efforts. For instance GOPAC developed a Code of Conduct for MPs, published a *Handbook for Parliamentarians on Curbing Corruption* and more recently a *Handbook for Legislators on Congressional Oversight in Presidential Systems,* and has also provided peer support programs by encouraging the development of national chapters comprising reform-minded members of parliament and by the global sharing of experience and lessons learned (see Campbell and Stapenhurst, 2005). In the course of some interviews conducted by one of the authors of this book, it was found that networks and regional association, in addition to providing MPs with a venue to meet like-minded MPs from other countries and share best practices and success stories, are among the most reliable, most important, and most effective sources of training for both parliamentarians and parliamentary staffers.

Through such networks, institutional frameworks have been strengthened to mitigate corruption. Regional and global conferences have facilitated the development of links between GOPAC and the UNDP, the Commonwealth Parliamentary Association and the International Association of Business and Parliament, among others.

CONCLUSIONS

For several years, scholars and practitioners have viewed parliaments as the representatives of society and as the institutional bodies that have the constitutional task of overseeing the executive. The international community has generally regarded legislative oversight as the appropriate institutional mechanism to ensure that executives are kept accountable for their actions, their expenditures, and their policy implementation. Furthermore, the international community has generally believed that the creation of a system of accountability in which executives explain and account to other institutions, to the citizens, and to various civil society groups, could play a key role in curbing corruption.

The studies produced over the course of the past 10 years have shown that effective oversight contributes to improving the quality, the functioning, the performance, and the legitimacy of a democratic regime (Pelizzo and Stapenhurst, 2012). They have also shown that effective oversight makes a significant contribution towards curbing corruption (Pelizzo and Stapenhurst, 2012), improving good governance (Stapenhurst, Pelizzo and Jacobs, 2013), and in securing the conditions for a more equitable distribution of resources (Pelizzo, 2012) and higher rates of growth and development.

In the first wave of studies on legislative oversight that were conducted at the request of several international organization, the effectiveness with which oversight was performed was equated to the number of oversight tools at the disposal of a legislature (Pelizzo and Stapenhurst, 2004), to the powers and the oversight mandate of a legislature, and to the context within which a legislature operates (for a review of the literature see Stapenhurst, 2011). In other words, all of these studies focused on static, structural, and mechanic conditions.

In a second wave of studies sparked by Stapenhurst (2011), the static, structural, and mechanic approach to the study of legislative oversight was complemented and integrated by what we could call, for lack of a better term, a dynamic approach to the study of oversight. Stapenhurst (2011) made clear that the effectiveness with which legislatures perform their oversight function reflects not only the powers and the tools at their disposal, but also the level of support and trust and confidence that they enjoy. Building on this work, Pelizzo and Stapenhurst (2012) have shown that voter trust is important for ensuring that legislative oversight activities are carried out effectively, because if legislatures lack the support of the population, they may not have the strength, the legitimacy, and the will to engage seriously in their oversight tasks. The key contribution of Pelizzo and Stapenhurst (2012) is precisely that of underlining the importance of political will for ensuring effective oversight and fighting corruption.

The purpose of this chapter was to show that while political will and trust are important for fighting corruption at the executive level, corruption (real or perceived) at the legislative level prevents legislatures from adequately performing their oversight tasks and fighting corruption. This is the reason why if legislatures are to fight corruption, they must rid themselves of corruption. The next two chapters are devoted to the steps that can be taken to reduce or eliminate legislative corruption and restore voter trust in the legislatures.

NOTES

1. Five waves of the World Value Survey have been conducted so far. They were administered in 1981, 1990, 1995–1998, 1999–2000, and 2005–2008. The data from the 2005–2008 survey are the ones that we will use in this chapter. On its website, the World Value Survey announced that a sixth wave is under way and will be completed by 2014.
2. In fact, if we remove the case of Vietnam from our sample, the average percentage of respondents reporting to have a great deal of confidence in parliament drops to 7.95. In other words, fewer than eight citizens out of ten report to have a great deal of confidence in their national legislature.
3. The two variables, as we will show later on, are fairly strongly related to but nonetheless quite different from one another. There is no evidence of collinearity, and there is no reason to believe that these two variables are measuring the same phenomenon. The Corruption Perception Index is computed on the basis of an elite survey, while the percentage of respondents declaring to have some or a lot of confidence in the legislature is computed on the basis of mass survey data. Hence, to be precise, the correlation analyses we are presenting here do not assess the relationship between the perceived corruption of a legislature and how strong the confidence in the legislature is, but between the level of perceived corruption of the legislature and the percentage of people reporting to have some or a lot of confidence in it.

4. One could of course, for theoretical reasons, assume that confidence in the legislature is a cause and not a consequence of the level of perceived corruption. In other words, one could assume that it is precisely because people have little trust in the legislature that they are more likely to believe it to be a corrupt institution. And one could, of course, and possibly with good reason, argue that the relationship between confidence in legislatures and the level of their perceived corruption could be best understood by employing simultaneous equation models. But while it is legitimate to assume that the arrow of causality runs in a different direction or runs in both directions, our purpose here was simply to show that if we assume the arrow of causality to run as we have in this chapter, an increase in the value of perceived corruption will lead to a decrease in the percentage of voters reporting to have confidence in the legislature.
5. A Canadian non-governmental organization.
6. With the founding of GOPAC, APNAC became one of GOPAC's constituent regional organizations; others including regional organizations in Latin America, the Middle East, and Asia.

REFERENCES

Campbell, M., and F. Stapenhurst. (2005). Developing Capacity through Networks: Lessons From Anticorruption Parliamentary Networks. *Capacity Development Briefs*, World Bank Institute Number 10.

Jain, A. K. (2001). *Political Economy of Corruption*. London: Routledge.

Lipset, S. M. (1959). Some Social Requisites of Democracy. *American Political Science Review*, LIII(1), 69–105.

Pelizzo, R. (2012). Strategie della crescita. Guida: Napoli.

Pelizzo, R., and R. Stapenhurst. (2004). Tools for Legislative Oversight Policy. *World Bank Research Working Paper*. Washington, D.C.: World Bank.

Pelizzo, R., and R. Stapenhurst. (2012). *Parliamentary Oversight Tools*. London: Routledge.

Stapenhurst, R. (2011). *Legislative Oversight and Curbing Corruption; Presidentialism and Parliamentarianism Revisited*. Unpublished PhD thesis. Canberra: Australian National University.

Stapenhurst, R., R. Pelizzo, and K. Jacobs. (2013). *Following the Money*. London: Pluto Press.

World Values Survey. (1981–2008). Official Aggregate v. 20090901, 2009. World Values Survey Association (www.worldvaluessurvey.org). Aggregate File Producer: ASEP/JDS, Madrid.

6   Legislative Ethics

INTRODUCTION

In this chapter, we discuss the link between public trust in parliament and the ethical behavior of MPs, noting that legislatures have lost legitimacy as the level of trust in parliament has fallen. There is a general belief that demonstrably more ethical behavior by MPs will enable legislatures to regain public trust. We observe that, in order to ensure more ethical behavior and to appeal to disgruntled voters, many parliaments are adopting ethics reforms—a set of norms and rules that are meant to guide MPs, prevent misconduct, reduce illicit behavior, and thereby restore the legitimacy of parliament in the public's eyes.

This chapter is organized in the following way. In the first section, after analyzing the survey data collected by the World Value Survey Association, we note that parliaments are, along with political parties, the least trusted political institutions in the world. This evidence, we go on to argue, can be used to illustrate what many regard as a parliamentary crisis. Parliaments no longer enjoy the level of legitimacy they once had and feel compelled to take some action to help regain some of this lost legitimacy. Since corruption and other forms of illicit and unethical behavior are believed to have been largely responsible for loss of legitimacy, parliaments have adopted ethics reforms as a way of regaining some legitimacy.

Building on these premises, in the second section we go on to discuss some of the steps legislatures have taken to regain the public trust. In doing so, we underline that, in addition to adopting specific measures to regulate the behavior of parliamentarians, parliaments also adopted specific measures to regulate the electoral process, an issue we examine in Chapter 7. While the adoption of electoral codes and party finance/campaign legislation was designed to regulate behavior of politicians in the electoral arena, the adoption of Codes of Ethics and Codes of Conduct was meant to regulate MPs' behavior in the legislative arena.

In the third section, we compare and contrast Codes of Ethics and Codes of Conduct. In doing so we note that Codes of Conduct differ from Codes of Ethics on two grounds: First, they are more specific and, second, they

establish sanctions for violations of their dispositions. Building on this discussion, in the fourth section we provide an in-depth analysis of the dispositions of several Codes of Conduct. This comparative analysis illustrates an
important point, namely that in spite of their variation (in length and specificity) nearly all Codes of Conduct provide some guidance on a fairly small
number of areas. In the fifth section, we discuss some of the conditions that
may favor the successful enforcement of a Code of Conduct, while in the
sixth and final section, we formulate some tentative conclusions.

ETHICS AND TRUST

Over the past 32 years, the World Value Survey Association has conducted five
waves of survey investigations to monitor the political, cultural and ideologi-
cal attitudes of citizens worldwide.[1] Respondents to these surveys were asked,
among other things, to indicate whether they had a great deal, quite a lot, not
very much, or no confidence whatsoever in a number of key institutions.

From the responses, it emerged quite clearly that, political parties aside,
legislatures are the most distrusted institutions.[2] The analysis of responses—
shown in Table 6.1—makes it clear that respondents have more confidence
in the Church, the education system, the armed forces, television, the police,
the government, and the civil service than they have in parliament, labor
unions, and political parties.

Table 6.1   Confidence and Institutions

Institution	Percentage of respondents reports to have		Total of respondents
	A great deal	Quite a lot	
Education system	32.2	35.7	67.9
Churches	34.0	32.4	66.4
Armed forces	23.4	41.0	64.4
Police	17	41.3	58.3
Television	12.2	37.6	49.8
Government	14.1	33.5	47.6
Civil service	8.8	36.9	45.7
Press	9.4	34.8	44.2
Parliament	10.2	29.5	39.7
Labor union	7.7	31.4	39.1
Political parties	6.1	21.1	27.2

Source: World Values Survey 1981–2008 Official Aggregate v.20090901, 2009. World Values
Survey Association (www.worldvaluessurvey.org). Aggregate File Producer: ASEP/JDS, Madrid.

In fact, only 39.7 and 27.2 percent of the respondents had either a great deal or quite a lot of confidence in Parliament and political parties, respectively. By contrast, the percentage of respondents that had either a great deal or quite a lot of confidence in the education system was 67.9 percent, in the Church 66.4 percent, in the armed forces 64.4 percent, in television 49.8 percent, in the police 58.3 percent, in the government 47.6 percent, in the civil service 45.7 percent, and in the press 44.2 percent.

There is a strong, negative, and significant relationship between confidence in political institutions and their perceived corruption; as we can see from Figure 6.1, institutions that are perceived to be most corrupt are the ones in which the smallest percentage of respondents report to have a great deal of confidence.[3]

There is also a clearly detectable negative relationship between the percentage of respondents who have quite a lot of confidence in an institution and the percentage of respondents who perceive an institution to be the most corrupt. See Figure 6.2.

Not surprisingly, when we correlate the total confidence in various institutions with their perceived corruption, we find that they are inversely related. Confidence is highest when perceived corruption is lowest and vice versa. See Figure 6.3.

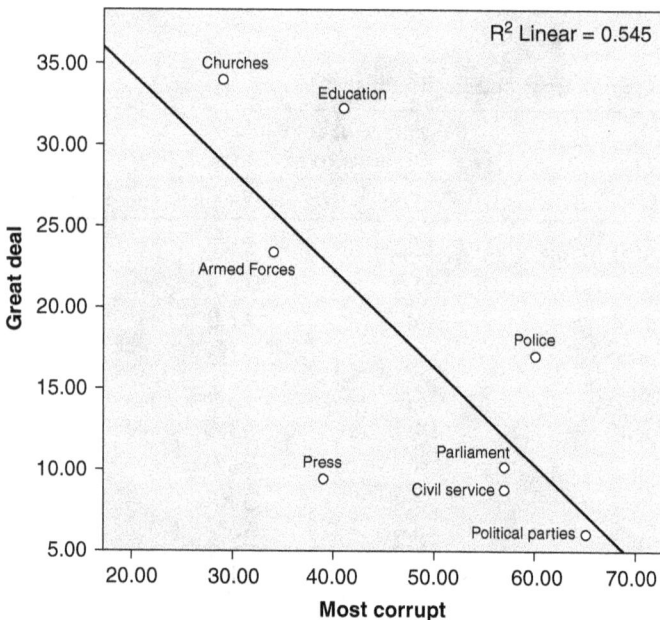

Figure 6.1   Perceived Corruption and "Great Deal" of Confidence

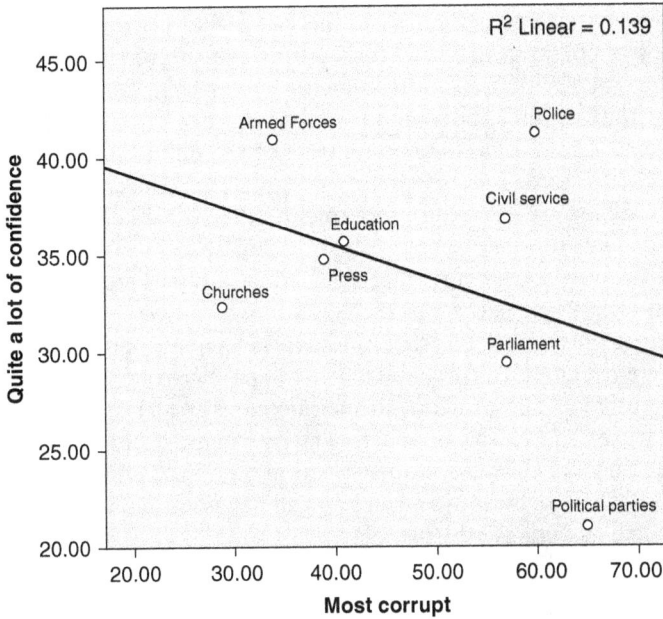

Figure 6.2   Perceived Corruption and "Quite a Lot" of Confidence

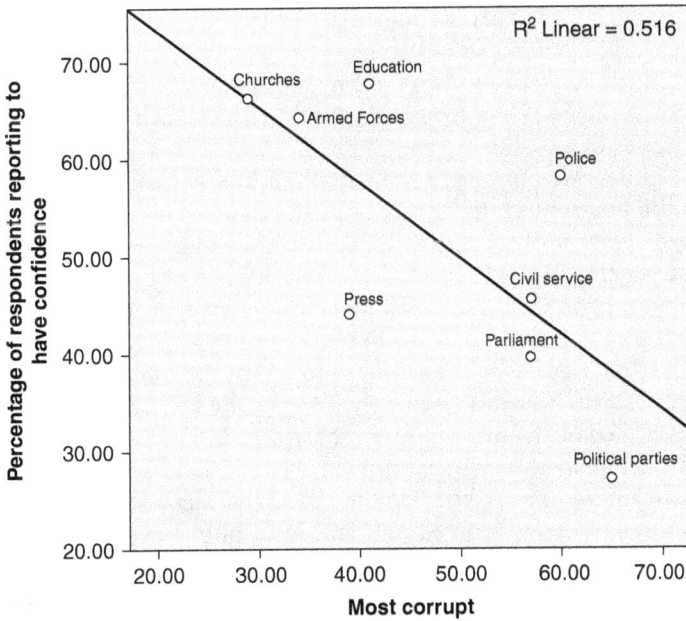

Figure 6.3   Confidence and Perceived Corruption

This evidence is consistent with the claim that corruption, or just the perception of corruption, erodes the legitimacy of a given institution—hence the need to take some steps to regain citizen trust.

The initiatives and, more importantly, the regulations that legislatures have undertaken to regain the confidence of the public can be divided into two categories. Some initiatives and/or regulations concern the behavior of MPs *before* they are elected to parliament, while others concern the behavior of MPs *after* they are elected to parliament.

In the first respect, we note that legislatures and parliaments have enacted campaign legislation, party finance legislation, and electoral codes to ensure that elections are free and fair, that candidate behavior is both legal and ethical, and that contributions to party and individual politician campaigns are scrupulously monitored.[4] These factors are considered in greater detail in Chapter 7.

Legislatures have also taken active steps to ensure that the behavior of MPs after they are elected and their election has been ratified is also ethical. Since these steps are meant to ensure ethical behavior in parliament, they are often labeled as "ethics reforms."

ETHICS REFORMS

Ethics reforms, such as the adoption of a Code of Ethics or of a Code of Conduct, were first enacted in the private sector (Fiorini, 2003). In fact, when companies and corporations realized that they could lose significant portions of their market shares if they were perceived to tolerate unscrupulous and unethical behavior by their managers and staff, they took care to protect their image by implementing ethics reforms such as Codes of Ethics and/or Codes of Conduct.

These codes were meant to serve both an internal and an external function. In the first respect, they were designed to provide behavioral guidance to the managers, workers, and employees by clarifying what type of behavior could be regarded as acceptable and what kind was unacceptable. At the same time, they were also designed to set a standard by which the company could and should be judged by the public, which could otherwise have unreasonable expectations as to the standard to which the company should abide.

Ethics reforms were subsequently adopted by the public sector. Public services, city councils, justices, and legislatures eventually decided to enact reforms similar to those in the private sector. The evidence presented by political scientists leaves little doubt about the fact that where such ethics reforms have been adopted and enforced, public perception of unethical behavior has markedly declined (Stapenhurst and Pelizzo, 2006; Bruce, 1996). This decline can be ascribed in part to the fact that citizens now have a clearer understanding of what is ethical behavior in the public sphere and also of the fact that such reforms provided guidance to public officials about what is appropriate behavior and what is not.

CODES OF ETHICS AND CODES OF CONDUCT

Experts have generally agreed that the term "ethics reforms" can be employed to indicate Codes of Ethics, Codes of Conduct, ethics rules, and/ or all the above (Bruce, 1996; Stapenhurst and Pelizzo, 2006). While there is general agreement that the adoption of Codes of Conduct, Codes of Ethics, and ethics rules are ethics reforms that may be beneficial for the promotion of good governance, there is less agreement on the exact meaning of each of these concepts.

For instance, some experts have suggested that Codes of Ethics are very specific sets of ethical dispositions, that they provide clear behavioral guidance, and that they establish sanctions for clear violations of the code itself, whereas Codes of Conduct are very vague and aspirational documents (National Democratic Institute, 1999).

A second group of experts has instead suggested that while some colleagues go to great lengths to explain why and how Codes of Conduct differ from Codes of Ethics, there is no real difference between Codes of Ethics and Codes of Conduct for they are one and the same thing (Gilman, 2005).[5]

A third position was suggested by Ann Fiorini (2003), who argued that the only reason why there is confusion between Codes of Ethics and Codes of Conduct is that most people do not understand what a Code of Ethics really is and therefore they pass legislation that they consider to be a "Codes of Ethics," while it should instead be regarded as a code a of conduct.

A fourth position was presented by Willa Bruce (1996) and Andrew Brien (1999). These scholars have argued in their work that there is a big difference between Codes of Ethics and Codes of Conduct. Codes of Ethics, they argue, are aspirational documents that state the institutional values and, in doing so, represent a sort of quality assurance to the public. Codes of Conduct, by contrast, "are more concrete and practical . . . they represent executive orders or legislatively defined and enforceable behavioral standards with sanction for violation" (Bruce, 1996, p. 24). In other words, Codes of Conduct differ from Codes of Ethics in three respects: they are more precise, they are concrete and practical, and they sanction violations of the code.

The presence/absence of sanctions for possible violations of the dispositions of a code is the key indicator of whether a document is a Code of Conduct or a Code of Ethics. As Fiorini (2003) made clear, Codes of Ethics do not sanction "violation of their provisions."

LEGISLATIVE CODES OF CONDUCT

Given their legitimacy crisis and the fact that parliamentarians may not always have a shared understanding of whether an action is ethical or not (Allen, 2008; Mancuso, 1995; Pelizzo and Ang, 2008a; Pelizzo and Ang, 2008b), many legislatures have taken active steps to set behavioral standards for their members in the hope of regaining public confidence. They have generally done so by enacting ethics reforms.

Ethics reforms were implemented and ethics rules were introduced in a large number of countries as evidenced by the data collected by the Inter-Parliamentary Union (IPU) in 2009 and, more recently, by the European Parliament (2011). For instance, ethics rules can be found in Bahrain, Bhutan, Canada, Chile, Georgia, Germany, Indonesia, Ireland, Japan, Kenya, Korea, Latvia, the Philippines, Poland, Singapore, Spain, Uganda, the United Kingdom, and the United States. In the majority of these cases, legislatures drafted and adopted Codes of Conduct for legislators and, in some cases, for legislative staff as well. Empirical analyses revealed that while these Codes of Conduct are all considerably more specific than Codes of Ethics would be, there is nonetheless considerable variation in how specific the dispositions of the adopted Codes of Conduct are.

For instance, Chapter 25 of the *National Assembly Bill of the Kingdom of Bhutan 2008* devoted its 24 articles to regulating the behavior of MPs: Sixteen were devoted to their behavior in parliament, six dealt with incompatibilities and ineligibility, three dealt with conflicts of interest (and the prevention thereof), and two articles detailed how MPs could bring complaints before the legislature. In terms of content, the Code of Conduct provided clear dispositions with regard to information that it is not in the public domain, gifts, donations, awards, decorations from foreign countries, and the disclosure of interests.

In Chile, the Code of Conduct contains 14 articles and three transitional dispositions divided into five sections plus the one pertaining to the transitional disposition. The first and the second part of the Code that deal respectively with the general norms and duties of MPs are very similar to the dispositions one would read in a Code of Ethics rather than in a Code of Conduct. However, the dispositions listed in the third section dealing with prohibitions display precisely the kind of specificity and detail that one expects to find in a Code of Conduct. This section forbids MPs to use the information acquired in their public role to achieve private gain, to draft legislation from which they would benefit, to use their public title for personal benefit, to sell goods that were entrusted to them for the performance of the public role, or to distort the functioning of the legislature. The fourth section states that a nine-member committee of legislators, the Committee of Conduct (Comision de Conducta), must be created at the beginning of each legislature to administer the Code and to sanction violations thereof.

In Kenya, the Codes of Ethics and the Code of Conduct were established by *The Public Officer Ethics Act*. The 42 articles of this act are divided into six sections—the introduction; the specific Codes of Conduct and ethics; general Codes of Conduct and ethics; the declaration of income, assets and liabilities; the enforcement of the codes; and some final provisions. This law establishes a broad framework for ensuring that members of the public sector behave in an ethical manner. With regard to MPs, it establishes that the ethics committee of the National Assembly is responsible for the ethical behavior of parliamentarians. It is the duty of the committee to adopt and enforce a Code of Ethics and a Code of Conduct, the dispositions of which must include all the requirements listed in the third part of the law. These requirements concern the need to act always in a professional manner, to respect the rule of law, to avoid using the public function to achieve personal gains, not to act solely in the interest of a foreign nation, to preserve the public confidence in the institutions, to refrain from sexual harassment, and to declare personal interests. The ethics committee has the authority to go beyond the dispositions and the prescriptions listed in the third part of this law and add additional dispositions. The Public Officer Ethics act serves two additional functions. First, it provides MPs with considerable detail as to how they should disclose their interests, assets, and liabilities as well as to the sanctions that can be imposed for violations of the dispositions listed in this act. Second, it provides ethics committees with clear guidelines as to how they should perform their tasks.

In Latvia, the dispositions of the Code of Conduct are detailed in the *Law on the Prevention of Conflict of Interest in Activities of Public Officials*. This law, which consolidates several pieces of legislation enacted between 2003 and 2010, is divided into 30 sections dealing respectively with restrictions on employment, income, commercial activities, gifts, donations, additional payments and the use of information gathering while performing public duty. This law prohibits members from participating in the drafting, voting, and approving of parliamentary acts from which they or their relatives can derive personal benefit, economic or otherwise. Similarly, members are forbidden from attempting to influence the drafting or the adoption of a parliamentary act from which they could benefit. Additional dispositions pertain to declaration of interests and the sanctions that may be applied to MPs who violate the dispositions of this law. While all these dispositions, with their detailed listing of what MPs can or should do, are precisely the dispositions that characterize Codes of Conduct, the dispositions stated in Article 22 of the *Law on Prevention of Conflict of Interest* are precisely the kind of dispositions that characterize a Code of Ethics. These dispositions are not practical, they are not specific, they do not state sanctions, and they are rather aspirational in character. The importance of this Latvian law, for the present purposes, is due to the fact that it makes clear that Codes of Ethics and Codes of Conduct are not incompatible, they can co-exist, and more importantly, that the dispositions of the Code of Ethics can be included, usually as a preamble, into the larger, more detailed body of a Code of Conduct.

In Uganda, the Code of Conduct is a fairly brief appendix (Appendix F) to the otherwise fairly detailed Standing Orders. The Code is divided into two parts. The first part, comprising Articles 1 to 5, is fairly aspirational in tone: It invites MPs to be selfless, accountable, objective, open, and leaders. From Article 6 onwards, the dispositions are more specific as they require MPs not to accept bribes, to declare their interests, to avoid conflicts of interests, to disclose any interest they may have before engaging in any activity, not to act as paid advocates, and not to use information obtained while performing parliamentary duty.

There is considerable variation in how detailed Codes of Conduct and their provisions are. Some pay particular attention to gifts, while others provide more detailed disposition with regard to travel. The German Code of Conduct has a specific rule or article on lawyers. Rule 2 of the Code of Conduct for members of the Bundestag (lower chamber) establishes that if a member of parliament is a lawyer and he/she is representing the German Federal Republic in or outside the court for a fee, he/she shall inform the president of the chamber in case the fee exceeds a certain value set by the president of the chamber. Similarly this rule establishes that if a member is a lawyer representing a third party (in court or outside court) against the German Federal Republic, he/she will have to disclose such representation if the fee exceeds the amount established by the president of the chamber. The norms of code can vary considerably in how detailed they can be.

The differences across codes are due to the fact that legislatures and legislators are confronted with different conditions in different countries and the ethical dispositions, the ethics codes, and the Code of Conduct need to adjust to the specific conditions under which they are expected to operate. In spite of these, the vast majority of Codes of Conduct provide some behavioral guidance in a fairly limited number of areas. Specifically, nearly all Codes of Conduct make recommendations on a fairly small number of areas, which include: gifts, travel, employment, compensation, fees, honoraria, nepotism, the use of confidential information, conflict of interests, the abuse of power, and the use of a public position to receive a personal gain.

Most ethics reforms or ethics rules require MPs to disclose and in several instances register their interests. The vast majority of codes that contain disclosure dispositions ask MPs to disclose their interests with regard to tax returns, sources of patrimonial income, investments, sources of income/ business of the partner, shares, ownership of a business, real estate interest, offices and directorships held, indebtedness, liabilities, contracts with public entities, fees and honoraria, professional licenses, reimbursement of travel expenses, deposits in financial institutions, professional services rendered, and names and interests of immediate family members.

THE SUCCESS OF THE CODES

The examples discussed above illustrate that ethics rules and Codes of Conduct are institutionalized in a fairly limited number of ways. In some instances, ethics rules and Codes of Conduct were included in laws and legislative proposals that aimed to regulate the behavior of public officials, while in other cases ethics rules and Codes of Conduct were included in parliamentary standing orders or rules of procedures.

The oversight literature has long discussed whether the way in which an institution is created affects its success or not. For instance, in their global analysis of what makes Public Accounts Committees work effectively, Stapenhurst, Pelizzo, and Jacobs (2013) have reported that there are two main positions in the literature: Some experts have argued that these committees are most effective when they are created by a constitutional disposition, while others have argued instead that they are most effective when they are created by an Act of Parliament, for this act testifies to the parliament's willingness and desire to make the PAC work effectively.

To the best of our knowledge, no study on legislative ethics and Codes of Conduct has addressed whether a Code of Conduct is more effective when it is part of a law regulating the behavior of public officials or when it is part of the parliamentary rules. Research suggests, however, that the successful adoption and enforcement of the dispositions of a Code of Conduct depends to a large extent on whether there is a common political culture, which is a common set of political attitudes, values, and standards. The pioneering work of Skelcher and Snape (2001) in this respect suggested that the success of a Code of Conduct depends on three basic conditions, namely

1) Whether the individuals that the code is supposed to regulate share attitudes and values,
2) Whether they have a shared understanding of the problems that the code is supposed to address, and
3) Whether they have a shared understanding of how these problems may be addressed and possibly resolved.

Empirical analyses performed over the years (Mancuso, 1993 and 1995; Pelizzo and Ang, 2008a and 2008b; Allen 2008) have shown that the ethical attitudes are far from being homogeneous. But, while the absence of homogeneous attitudes towards right and wrong, of a homogeneous understanding of what is appropriate conduct for an MP, and of a shared understanding of what are the ethical dilemmas confronting the legislature make it more challenging for a legislature or a legislative committee to draft, approve, and enforce a Code of Conduct, there is some reason to believe that it is precisely under these circumstances that the guidance a code may provide is particularly useful.

If MPs already agree on what is appropriate, permissible, and acceptable, the guidance that a Code of Conduct or an ethics committee may provide may be redundant. Conversely, if MPs do not agree on what represents appropriate conduct, the guidance provided by a code or by an ethics committee is useful and possibly essential in ensuring that MPs behave in a responsible and ethical manner. At the extreme, however, where there is no agreement at all among MPs on what is ethical behavior, the administration and the enforcement of a Code of Conduct may be quite challenging.[6]

CONCLUSIONS

Ethics reforms, such as the adoption of Codes of Ethics and Codes of Conduct, are intended to curb corruption, prevent unethical behavior, and restore the public trust in parliament.

Ethics reforms are meant to work by making it increasingly harder for parliamentarians to engage in unethical behavior and by establishing severe sanctions for those who engage in unethical behavior. In fact, MPs who engage in such behavior may be sanctioned with reprimands, fines, reductions of salary, and suspensions from office. Ethics reforms also represent a clear signal for voters that legislatures will not tolerate unethical behavior by parliamentarians.

Important as ethics reforms such as the adoption of disclosure rules and Codes of Conduct really are, their success is often hindered by some obstacles. The first is that the codes are not written with sufficient clarity. Sometimes a dispassionate reader after reading several times the dispositions of the code is not sure whether a certain behavior is always acceptable, is sometimes acceptable, is generally unacceptable, or is absolutely forbidden. The dispositions concerning "gifts" are a case in point. In some instances, after the reader has been informed that accepting gifts is absolutely forbidden, he/she is given a rather long and detailed list of exceptions, and he/she may no longer be sure whether there is any type of gift that is actually forbidden. In other instances, the dispositions concerning "gifts" are so poorly drafted that the reader is left with the impression that while cheap gifts must not be accepted by MPs, extremely expensive gifts can instead be accepted—which is precisely what restrictions on gifts are generally meant to prevent. If the dispositions of a Code of Conduct are not formulated with some clarity, it is very hard to enforce them. Hence, it is very important that Codes of Conduct are written as clearly as possible. The second obstacle is that the dispositions of some Codes of Conduct are totally unreasonable, unrealistic and, as a result, cannot possibly be enforced. Hence it is essential that the Code of Conduct sets a standard that MPs can respect.

Legislatures should not simply adopt clear and reasonable ethical dispositions, they should also enforce them in a consistent and impartial way. The partial, inconsistent, partisan administration and enforcement of the code will inevitably ensure the failure of the newly established ethics regime.

NOTES

1. The World Value Survey data can be found at the following link www. wvsevsdb.com/wvs/WVSData.jsp.
2. Party crisis has been documented in the political science literature for the past 15 years. One of the most compelling explanations provided for why parties no longer enjoy the level of legitimacy they once had is due to the fact that they are perceived to be completely detached from reality, to be detached from their

voters, and to act as a self-interested cartel. A comprehensive discussion of this literature can be found in Pelizzo (2008).

3. The data on the perceived corruption of specific institutions are taken from Transparency International's Corruption Barometer.

4. On party political funding and on the efforts made to curb corruption by regulating campaign and political finance, see Pinto-Duschinsky (2006).

5. Gilman (2005, p. 4) went on to argue that "Ethics codes or codes of conduct seldom provide detailed, specific prohibitions. Rather, they are broader sets of principles that are designed to inform specific laws or government actions;" it is clear that he regards ethics codes and codes of conduct as one and the same thing both in nominal and in substantive terms.

The GOPAC Global Task Force on Parliamentary Ethics and Conduct specified the need for an ethics and conduct regime to be more all-encompassing. *See* Power, G. *Handbook on Parliamentary Ethics and Conduct a Guide for Parliamentarians.* Global Organization of Parliamentarians Against Corruption and Westminster Foundation for Democracy. 2009.

6. The GOPAC PEC guide offers suggestions on how MPs can work toward developing a shared understanding of these concepts.

REFERENCES

Allen, N. (2008). A New Ethical World of British MPS? *Journal of Legislative Studies*, 14(3), 297–314.

Brien, A. (1999). A Code of Conduct for Parliamentarians? *Research Paper 2*, Department of Parliamentary Library of Australia.

Bruce, W. (1996). Codes of Ethics and Codes of Conduct: Perceived Contribution to the Practice of Ethics in Local Government. *Public Integrity Annual*, 23–29.

European Parliament. (2011). *Parliamentary Ethics: A Question of Trust.* Office for the Promotion of Parliamentary Democracy,

Fiorini, A. (2003). Business and Global Governance: The Growing Role of Corporate Codes of Conduct. *Brookings Review*, (2) 4–8.

Gilman, S. C. (2005). Ethics Codes and Codes of Conduct as Tools for Promoting an Ethical and Professional Public Service. Paper prepared for PREM, the World Bank, Washington D.C. Available at: www.oecd.org/mena/governance/35521418.pdf

Mancuso, M. (1993). Ethical Attitudes of British MPs. *Parliamentary Affairs*, 46(2), 179–191.

Mancuso, M. (1995). *The Ethical World of British MPs.* Quebec City: McGill-Queen University Press.

National Democratic Institute. (1999). LEGISLATIVE ETHICS: A Comparative Analysis. *Legislative Research Paper*, 4.

Pelizzo, R. (2008). *Cartel Parties and Cartel Party Systems.* Saarbruecken, Verlag: Doctor Mueller.

Pelizzo, R., and B. Ang. (2008a). An Ethical Map of Indonesian MPs. *Public Integrity*, 10(3), 253–272.

Pelizzo, R., and B. Ang. (2008b). A Code of Conduct for Indonesia: Problems and Perspectives. *Parliamentary Affairs*, 61(2), 315–333.

Pinto-Duschinsky, M. (2006). Party Political Funding. In Rick Stapenhurst, Niall Johnston, and Riccardo Pelizzo (Eds.) *The Role of Parliament in Curbing Corruption*, pp. 187–196. Washington: World Bank.

Power, G. (2009). Handbook on Parliamentary Ethics and Conduct a Guide for Parliamentarians. Global Organization of Parliamentarians Against Corruption and Westminster Foundation for Democracy.

Skelcher C., and S. Snape (2001). Ethics and Local Councillors: Modernising Standards of Conduct. *Parliamentary Affairs* 54; pp. 72-87

Stapenhurst, R., and R. Pelizzo. (2006). Legislative Ethics and Codes of Conduct. In Rick Stapenhurst, Niall Johnston, and Riccardo Pelizzo (Eds.) *The Role of Parliament in Curbing Corruption,* pp. 197–205. Washington: World Bank.

Stapenhurst, R., R. Pelizzo, and K. Jacobs. (2013). *Following the Money.* London, Pluto Press.

World Values Survey. (1981–2008). Official Aggregate v. 20090901, 2009. World Values Survey Association (www.worldvaluessurvey.org). Aggregate File Producer: ASEP/JDS, Madrid.

7 Political Finance

INTRODUCTION

Electoral campaigns are at the heart of democracy. Without elections, there is no representation, and without representation there is no democracy. Over the years, however, the cost of electoral campaigning, both for parties and candidates, has increased as because of social, sociological, political, institutional, and technological reasons.

Voters have found new forms of political participation, and they can express their political views without having to join political parties. As a result, political parties can no longer count on their membership base. In addition, the cost of political advertising has increased. The combination of these developments has led to a marked increase in the cost of electoral campaigning.

Political party finance specialists, such as Michael Pinto-Duschinsky (2002), have argued that rising campaign costs (along with the declining political party revenue from membership fees) have placed considerable pressure on both political parties and candidates to find additional sources of funding. One such source is through electoral corruption, which is one of the sub-types of legislative corruption, as we noted in Chapters 1 and 3. In other words, electoral (or campaign) corruption—where political parties and candidates seek illicit contributions to cover their campaign costs—is viewed as one of the consequences of the rising costs of campaigning.

Given the rising costs of electoral campaigning, various dispositions have been introduced to regulate what can broadly be defined as political party finance. Such dispositions have been introduced to regulate the revenue and expenditures of parties and candidates.[1]

In this chapter, we assess how much the world of political finance regulations has changed in the course of a decade since the publication of Pinto-Duschinsky's classic work (2002). In doing so, we will analyze the data collected by International IDEA on party income, expenditure, public funding, reporting, and sanctions.

This chapter is organized in a fairly straightforward way. Since the work of Pinto-Duschinsky (2002) opened up this area of inquiry, presented a considerable wealth of empirical information, and set the stage for nearly all subsequent studies on these and related topics, in the first section we provide a summary of his key findings. In section two, we discuss the contribution bans and the limits on party income. In doing so, specific attention is paid to whether, how, and to what extent anonymous donations, corporate donations, and foreign donations are banned in the countries for which International IDEA collected information. Specific attention is also paid to the limits that may be imposed on contributions to party finance. Section three discussed the various provisions that have been adopted worldwide to provide political parties with public funds with the hope that by reducing the amount of financial resources needed by political parties, the parties would be less inclined to seek illicit funding. Section four discusses the regulations on party spending, which were introduced to curb parties' financial needs. Section five discusses the regulation on party finance reporting, on how party finance is overseen, and on how violations of party finance legislation are sanctioned. Finally, in the last section, we formulate some conclusions, and we suggest that political will is an essential and necessary condition for eliminating or at least curbing electoral corruption.

ONCE UPON A TIME

Pinto-Duschinsky (2002) reported on political party finance regulations and subsidies in a sample of 104 countries.[2] In this analysis, he showed that some regulations were more common than others, that some types of contributions were banned, that contributions and spending were limited, that political parties and other political organizations received various types of public subsidies, and that, overall, the world of party and campaign finance was phenomenally under-regulated.

According to Pinto-Duschinsky (2002), disclosure rules were the most common regulations, and yet they were found only in 62 percent of the countries (see Table 7.1). A ban on foreign donations was enacted in less than 50 percent, spending limits in only 41 percent, the (partial or complete) disclosure of individual donors was required in 32 percent, contributions limits were enforced in 28 percent, and the complete ban on corporate political donations was enforced in only 8 percent of the cases.

Leaving complete bans on corporate donations aside, which are quite rare, even the most common regulations were not particularly widespread. In fact, bans on foreign donations did not exist in more than 50 percent of the countries included in the Pinto-Duschinsky study, spending limits did not exist in nearly 60 percent, donors were not disclosed in nearly 70 percent, and contribution limits did not exist in more than 70 percent. An overwhelming majority of countries also lacked the most common regulations

Table 7.1 Regulations on Political Party Finance

Regulation	Percentage of responding countries having this regulation
Disclosure rules of any kind (any)	62
Ban on foreign donations (partial or complete)	49
Spending limits (any)	41
Disclosure of individual donors (partial or complete)	32
Contribution limits (any)	28
Ban on corporate political donations (partial or complete)	16
Ban on corporate political donations (complete)	8

Source: Pinto-Duschinsky (2002)

regarding campaign and party finance and, not surprisingly, the least common regulations were almost nowhere to be found.

International IDEA generated political finance databases in 2003 and 2012. This database, which covers 180 countries, is divided into four areas: bans and limits on income, the presence/absence of funding, the regulation of spending, and the reporting/oversight of party finance.

By analyzing these data, we are able to assess how well political party finance is now regulated and to track how much the world of political party finance regulation has changed over the past decade, since the publication of Pinto-Duschinsky's (2002) study.

CONTRIBUTION BANS AND LIMITS ON POLITICAL PARTY INCOME

In his analysis, Pinto-Duschinsky (2002) separated regulations pertaining to political party income and expenditure from public subsidies. The regulations concerning political party income and expenditure were, in turn, subdivided into two categories: bans and limits.[3] Political party income bans, as defined by Pinto-Duschinsky, concerned foreign donations, paid election advertising on television, and corporate political donations, whereas limits related to the contributions. The International IDEA dataset covers a much larger number of items and provides a considerably more precise information; it separates bans and limits that apply to contributions to political party finances over time (other than for an election), to party electoral or campaign finance, and to candidates' campaign finance.

Bans on Donations

Except for disclosure rules that were found in 62 percent of the cases, Pinto-Duschinsky reported that the single most common regulation was the (partial or complete) ban on foreign donations—a regulation that existed in nearly half of the countries. The International IDEA data show that this kind of regulation is still one of the most common, with a ban on foreign donations to political parties existing in 66.8 percent of reporting countries (113 of 169) and that a ban on foreign donations to candidates exists in 51.8 percent (85 of 164). Further details are presented in Table 7.2.

The ban on corporate donations for both parties and candidates is considerably less common. In fact, the ban on corporate donations to parties exists only in 22 percent (38 of 170) of countries that provided some information, while the ban on corporate donations to parties exists only in 38 of 165 reporting countries. While in a large majority of cases corporate donations are permitted, the data presented in Table 7.3 show that the number and the percentage of countries adopting this kind of regulation is higher than what Pinto-Duschinsky had reported. While Pinto-Duschinsky reported that a complete ban on this type of donation existed only in 8 percent of the cases and a partial or complete ban existed in 16 percent of the cases, the data presented Table 7.3 (column 5) show that the percentage of countries adopting this type of regulation is much more common than it used to be. In 22.3 (38 out of 170) percent of the countries included in the sample, corporate donations to parties are banned, while corporate donations to candidates are banned in 23 percent (38 out of 165) of cases.

The International IDEA data also show, surprisingly, that in a majority of cases there is no ban on donations to parties and candidates from corporations that have government contracts: Such a ban exists in only in 79 of 168 (47 percent) reporting countries, while a ban on such contributions to candidates exists in only 63 of 162 (38.8 percent) reporting countries. This means that while political parties in nearly half of the countries are not allowed to be financed by corporations that have government contracts,

Table 7.2   Ban on Foreign Donations

	1	2	3	4	5
	Number of countries where the ban exists	Number of countries where the ban does not exist	Number of countries that did not provide information	Number of valid answers	Percentage of valid answers where the ban exists
Parties	113	56	11	169	66.8
Candidates	85	79	16	164	51.8

Table 7.3 Ban on Corporate Donations

	1	2	3	4	5
	Number of countries where the ban exists	Number of countries where the ban does not exist	Number of countries that did not provide evidence	Number of valid answers	Percentage of valid answers where the ban exists
Parties	38	132	10	170	22.3
Candidates	38	127	15	165	23.0

Table 7.4 Ban on Donations from Corporations with Government Contracts

	1	2	3	4	5
	Number of countries where the ban exists	Number of countries where the ban does not exist	Number of countries that did not provide evidence	Number of valid answers	Percentage of valid answers where the ban exists
Parties	79	89	12	168	47.0
Candidates	63	99	18	162	38.8

candidates can receive this type of contribution in more than 60 percent of the countries. See Table 7.4.

Many countries now ban anonymous donations to both political parties and candidates. Such donations to parties are banned in 88 of the 163 (53.9 percent) reporting countries but are allowed with some limitations in 22 (13.4 percent) such countries and are allowed without limitations in the remaining 53 (33 percent) countries. Anonymous donations to candidates are banned in 66 countries (46.1 percent), limited in 17 countries (11.8 percent), and allowed in 60 countries (41.9 percent). Details are presented in Table 7.5.

Limits to Contributions

With regard to limits to parties' and candidates' ability to received funding, Pinto-Duschinsky (2002) noted that there were limits to contributions in only 28 percent of the cases. The International IDEA data distinguish between contributions that are given to political parties to help them campaign and contributions given to political parties over a given period of time. This distinction is important because a donor may not give anything to a political party in the course of an electoral campaign while handsomely

Table 7.5   Ban on Anonymous Donations

	1	2	3	4	5
	Number of countries where anonymous donations are banned	Number of countries where anonymous donations are allowed within limits	Number of countries where anonymous donations are allowed without limits	Number of valid answers	Percentage of valid answers where the ban exists
Parties	88	22	53	163	53.9
Candidates	66	17	60	143	46.1

Table 7.6   Limits on Contributions

To	Limits exist in (countries)	Limits do not exist (countries)	Total valid answers	Percentage where limits exist
Party over time	55	119	174	31.4
Party during elections	31 (+37)*	107	175	1.77 (38.8)**
Candidates	54	118	172	31.4

Legend: *The figure in parentheses illustrates the number of countries with a broader definition of the limits.** The figure in parentheses refers to the total number of countries, using both the narrow and broad definition of limits

funding the party for the rest of the year, in order to receive either material or symbolic rewards for his or her generosity.

With regard to the limits to donations over time, such limits exist only in 55 of 174 the countries (31.6 percent) that provided information, whereas the data concerning the limits on contributions given to political parties for their electoral efforts present a more complicated picture. There are such limits in 31 of the 175 reporting countries (17.7 percent), no limits in 107 countries (61.1 percent), and in 37 countries (21.1 percent), the limits placed on donations to political parties in the course of a campaign are the same limits set on regular donations. Contributions or donations to candidates are equally likely to be subjected to limits: Such limits exist in 54 of the 172 reporting countries. Computing the percentage of countries in which limits exist, as shown in Table 7.6, we can see that limits on donations/contributions to political parties over time exist in 55 countries (31.4 percent) and on donations/contributions to candidates in 54 countries (32 percent). More complicated is the assessment of how common the limits are to donations/contributions to parties in the course of electoral campaigns. In this respect, specific provisions exist only in 31 countries (18 percent), whereas in an additional 37 countries (21 percent), contributions or donations to political parties are subjected to the limits that are applied to donations and contributions to party finance over time. Hence, the total number of countries varies from 31 (17.7 percent) to 68 (38.8 percent), depending on whether we adopt a narrow or a broader understanding of the limits.

The evidence presented thus far leads to three basic conclusions. The first is that regulations, limits, and bans are not particularly common. The number of countries in which limits and bans exist are greatly outnumbered by the number in which they do not. Thus, there is a long way to go to adequately regulate the world of political finance. The second is that regulations are remarkably more common than they were a decade ago. The third is that, with one exception, parties and contributions to party finance are more likely to be regulated than candidates and contributions to candidates' campaigns. This is an area in which it is important, and possibly quite easy, to make some progress. It is important to adopt regulations because if this area is left unregulated, candidates, once elected, may be captive to the interests that financed their electoral campaign—thereby increasing legislative corruption. It would be quite easy to adopt regulations in this respect, since regulations already exist regarding contributions to political parties and these could quite easily be extended to political candidates.

PUBLIC FUNDING

Public funding has been introduced in various countries to compensate political parties for the expenses incurred in the course of electoral campaigns, finance their ordinary activities, cover part of their costs, reduce their need for money, and, perhaps above all, to prevent corruption.[4]

There are various ways in which the state can fund political parties. It can provide economic subsidies such as reimbursements for the electoral costs or subventions for financing parties' ordinary activities. It can provide parties with subsidies in kind and free broadcasting. In his analysis, Pinto-Duschinsky (2002) noted that free broadcasting could be found in 79 percent of the countries included in his analysis, direct public subsidies in 59 percent, and subsides in kind in 49 percent.

The International IDEA data cover some of the items discussed by Pinto-Duschinsky, neglect others, and provide information on new items. For example, the International IDEA data show that public funding to political parties is found in 117 of the reporting 177 countries (66.1 percent)—a considerable increase over what Pinto-Duschinsky (2002) had reported a decade earlier. Free or subsidized access to media for political parties exists in 119 of 171 (69.6 percent) of the countries, while free or subsidized access to media for candidates exists only in 84 of the reporting 168 countries (50 percent).

Legislators and institutional reformers had argued that the introduction of public contributions to political party finance would reduce political party financial needs and, as a consequence, reduce such parties' incentives to seek financial support from illicit sources. However, the record is not as successful as legislators and institutional reformers had hoped. Despite the introduction of generous party and campaign finance provisions, several scandals have occurred. Subsidizing political parties is not enough to satisfy their financial needs and to prevent illicit transactions. Rather, it is necessary to curb the costs of politics. This can be done by capping the level of parties and candidates' campaign expenses, which we will discuss in the next section, and by providing political parties and their candidates with in-kind subsidies and free political broadcasts. The evidence shows that the percentage of countries where parties can enjoy free broadcasts has declined, implying in all these cases that efforts to curb the costs of campaigning have failed.

REGULATIONS ON SPENDING

The data on regulations on spending are interesting. The first item concerns whether there is a ban on vote-buying. Such activity is banned in 161 of 170 (94.7 percent) of the countries that provided information and is allowed in only nine countries. These nine countries represent most regions of the world: Europe (Andorra, Czech Republic), Africa (Djibouti, Mauritania), the Middle East (Bahrain), and Central and South America (Argentina, Guatemala, Peru, and Venezuela).

These data have several implications, the most obvious of which is that there seems to be a strong relation between the existence of this ban and the form of government. In fact, seven of the nine countries that have not banned vote-buying have either a presidential (Argentina, Guatemala, Peru, Venezuela) or a semi-presidential system (Czech Republic, Djibouti, and Mauritania). Countries with a parliamentary form of government seem to be more conducive to the adoption of a ban on vote-buying. This may be one of the reasons heretofore overlooked: why average levels of corruption are lower in parliamentary systems than they are elsewhere (Stapenhurst, 2011; Pelizzo and Stapenhurst, 2012).

With regard to spending limits, Pinto-Duschinsky (2002) reported that such regulations existed in 41 percent of the countries. The data collected by International IDEA show a dramatic decline. In fact these limits exist only in 51 of 176 reporting countries (28.9 percent).

The evidence presented in this and in the previous section sustains the claim that efforts to curb the costs of political and electoral campaigning, and through these to minimize electoral corruption, have not enjoyed much success.

REPORTING, OVERSIGHT, AND SANCTIONS

In order to oversee, monitor, and scrutinize the political party finances, detect possible violations, and apply sanctions when necessary, political party finances must be disclosed.

Typically, political parties must report regularly on their finances, while both parties and candidates must also report on their campaign finances. Specifically, political parties must regularly report on their finances in 127 out of 171 reporting countries (74.3 percent), and they must also make a report on their electoral finances in 92 out of 173 reporting countries (53.2 percent). Candidates must report on their electoral finances in 103 out of 171 countries (60.1 percent). But while these reports must be submitted to the competent authorities, in a fairly high percentage of countries they are not made available to the public. In fact, provisions establishing that public disclosure exist only in 106 of 171 countries (61.9 percent), while they do not in the remaining 65 countries (38.1 percent).

While many institutions are, in various countries, mandated to perform this oversight task, the single most common oversight tools are electoral commissions, which oversee public finance in 50 of the 158 reporting countries (31.6 percent). Other institutions that have the task of overseeing political finance include: supreme audit institutions, courts of auditors (e.g., Andorra), constitutional councils (e.g., Algeria), federal judges (e.g., Argentina), audit service established by electoral commissions (e.g., Armenia), ministry of justice (e.g., Bahrain), management commission of parliament (e.g., Barbados), ministry of finance (e.g., Belgium), and ministry of interior (e.g., Cambodia)

Violations of the campaign or electoral finance legislation result in a plurality of sanctions. Of the 180 countries in the International IDEA dataset, 14 provided no data.[5] Of the remaining 166, one indicated that sanctions are not applicable (Vanuatu), seven reported that they do not employ sanctions, while the remaining countries employ various sanctions to punish violations.[6] Such sanctions vary in severity and in their distribution, with some being more common than others. For instance, fines are used in 132 countries (79.5 percent), imprisonment in 97 countries (58.4 percent), and loss of public funding in 61 countries (36.7 percent). Furthermore, 16 countries reported that violations are punished with the loss of the elected position, 50 respondents reported that violators must forfeit their seat, and 24 reported that violation is punished with loss of the nomination. Since loss of the elected office, forfeiture of the elected post, and loss of nomination are more or less equivalent, in 90 countries (54.2 percent) violation is punished with a loss of the seat. In 44 countries (26.5 percent), violation of results in either suspension or de-registration of a political party. See Table 7.7.

Table 7.7   Distribution of Sanctions (n = 166)

Sanction	Number of countries in which it is employed	Percentage
Fines	132	79.5
Imprisonment	97	58.4
Loss of public funding	61	36.7
Loss of elected position	16	9.6
Forfeiture of elected seat	50	30.1
Loss of nomination	24	14.4
Suspension or de-registration of a political party	44	26.5

The obvious implication of such a distribution of sanctions is that most countries—Dominican Republic, Madagascar, Malawi, Suriname, Swaziland, Sweden, Switzerland, and Vanuatu are the exceptions—adopt from a minimum of at least one sanction and up to a maximum of seven different sanctions. Hence, there is some variation in the range, number, and severity of sanctions that can be used to punish violations. Andorra adopts only one (loss of public funding), Angola adopts two (fines and prison), Albania adopts three (fines, loss of political funding, and loss of political rights), Bangladesh has four, Bhutan has five, Brazil adopts six, and the Democratic Republic of Congo adopts seven.

There is also considerable variation in the severity of sanctions. In some cases there are no sanctions, in other cases the violation of the legislation is punished with a fine, and in several cases it can be punished with the imprisonment of individuals and with suspension for parties.

CONCLUSIONS

In this chapter, we have assessed how much the world of political finance has changed in the course of the past decade. We did so by analyzing the data collected by International IDEA, and then by comparing the results with the findings of Pinto-Duschinsky (2002).

In addition to discussing the dispositions of political finance legislation pertaining to the limits and bans on sources of income and levels of expenditure, we paid attention to the dispositions concerning the reporting of income, its sources, the level of expenditures, and sanctions.

We now draw some conclusions as to how much the political finance legislation has changed, how much it has improved and in which areas it can be further improved. The first conclusion is that regulations are considerably more common than they were 10 years ago. Furthermore, it is clear that regulations concerning the party finances are more common than regulations concerning the campaign finance of individual candidates. We suggest that this is an area that needs to be better regulated. In several developing nations, political parties are not adequately institutionalized (and in some of the small Pacific island states, for example, political parties do not even exist, while elsewhere such parties may exist but lack the organization and the cohesion to discipline their candidates and their members), making it all the more important to establish clear, precise and enforceable dispositions to regulate the finances of candidates.

The second conclusion concerns public funding. In the course of a decade, the number of countries where public contributions are given to political party finances has increased, under the assumption that they reduce parties' financial needs and thus the risk of corruption. But the evidence in this respect is mixed, for no matter how much public money is given to political parties, their expenditures can always increase at a faster pace. Hence, the strategy that legislators and institutional reformers should focus on is to reduce the cost of politics rather than on providing more generous funding.

The cost of politics, and especially of campaigning, can be reduced by providing free political broadcasts and subsidies-in-kind, while at the same time placing stricter limits on the amount political parties and candidates can spend, especially during elections. In the first respect, the evidence is disappointing because the percentage of countries in which free political broadcast is provided has declined. In the second, the comparison of the data presented by Pinto-Duschinsky (2002) and those collected by International IDEA make it clear that the percentage of countries where limits on political expenditures exist has dramatically declined. In other words, efforts to curb the costs of politics have either not been made or have failed.

With regard to reports and sanctions, the evidence sustains the claim that most countries have adopted a wide range of provisions to ensure that political finances are overseen and that violations are punished. The question we are unable to answer is whether the existence of formal dispositions, formal institutions, and formal mechanisms are sufficient to deter political parties and candidates from engaging in corrupt activities or not. But we know from the legislative oversight literature that formal mechanisms (in this case, oversight tools and mechanisms) are insufficient to ensure oversight effectiveness. Rather, the effective use of oversight tools depends on the presence of the political will (Pelizzo and Stapenhurst, 2012). If we can extend this lesson to the field of political finance, then we can conclude that political will to oversee political finance is essential to ensure that political finance is overseen effectively.

Introducing more regulations, curbing the costs of politics and campaigning, and generating a political will to oversee political finance are three steps that must be taken to eradicate electoral corruption.

NOTES

1. The European legislators have devoted considerable attention to party finance legislation in recent decades. For example, the Belgian legislature enacted the law July 4, 1989; the French legislature enacted law n. 227 March 11, 1988, and n. 55 January 15, 1990, and their modifications; the German legislature, taking in the suggestions formulated by the German Constitutional Court in the *Bundesverfassunggericht* (issued on April 9, 1992) introduced new regulations governing party finance and the state contribution to party finance; the Spanish legislature enacted three major legislative pieces on party finance, namely organic law n. 3 July 2, 1987, organic law n. 5 June 19, 1985, and organic law n. 8 March 13, 1991. On German party finance and party finance legislation, see Gunlicks (1995), Poguntke (1995), Pulzer (2001) and Pelizzo (2004). In Great Britain, public contributions to party finance were initially introduced only for opposition parties (see the Resolution March 20, 1975, on Financial Assistance to Opposition Parties). British party finance legislation was then modified when the Representation of the People Act 1983 changed the dispositions the public contribution for parties' electoral expenses. Like the above-mentioned European legislatures, the Italian legislature has also devoted considerable attention to party finance. Law n. 195, enacted May 2, 1974, established a state contribution to finance parties' ordinary activities and also a reimbursement for parties' electoral expenses. The norms concerning the state contribution for parties' electoral expenses were then modified by laws n. 422 August 8, 1980, n. 659 November 18, 1981, n. 413 August 8, 1985, n. 515 December 10, 1993, n. 448 July 15, 1994, n. 43 February 23, 1995, and n. 309 July 27, 1995. Moreover, after the abrogation of articles 3 and 9 of law n. 195 May 2, 1974,—which abolished the state financial contribution for parties' ordinary activities—the Italian legislature introduced some new regulations on party finance. See Pelizzo (2004) and Pujas (2000).

2. Political party finance legislation can be divided into two broad sets of norms and dispositions that were meant to perform complementary tasks. On the one hand, party finance legislation introduces regulations that make it more difficult for individual candidates and political parties to be involved in electoral and campaign corruption. On the other hand, such legislation, by introducing or increasing state subsidies to political parties, is intended to provide political parties (and their candidates) with an incentive to not seek funds through illegal sources.

3. The French legislation on political party finance also recognizes that political parties can receive financial support from private sources. The modes of and limits to such contributions are fixed by article 11 of law n. 227, enacted March 11, 1988, as modified by law n. 55 of 1990, which establishes that political parties can collect funds exclusively through the intermediary action of a "mandataire," who can either be a physical person or an association, where the latter must be approved by the Commissione Nationale des comptes de campagne et des financements politiques. The French legislation rules that donations made by persons cannot exceed a certain limit and that donations from juridical persons, public companies, and foreign states are forbidden. In Germany, private contributions are governed by article 25 of the law passed by the Bundestag on January 1, 1994, which forbids contributions by political foundations, non-profit organizations, and religious organizations as well as by foreign citizens and anonymous donors. A peculiarity is that contributions are tax deductible (as they are in Canada). In Spain, the regulations

concerning private contributions are established by article 2 of organic law n. 3 of 1987, which fixes the limits and the modes of such contributions, bans foreign donations and donations from entities with government contracts, and establishes limits for anonymous donations and for donations from physical and juridical persons.

4. The record as to whether public funding of political parties has helped curb legislative corruption is mixed, at best. While generous party finance legislation had been enacted in various consolidated democracies (France, Germany, Italy, and Spain), major corruption scandals emerged in each of these countries. The best comparative analysis of the southern European cases was provided by Pujas and Rhodes (1999). On the German case see Scarrow (2006).

5. The 14 countries are: Bahamas, Barbados, Belize, Comoros, Djibouti, Equatorial Guinea, Grenada, Iraq, Liechtenstein, St. Kitts and Nevis, St. Vincent, Samoa, San Marino, and Tuvalu.

6. The seven countries reporting not to employ any sanction for violation of political finance legislation are the Dominican Republic, Madagascar, Malawi, Suriname, Swaziland, Sweden, and Switzerland.

REFERENCES

Gunlicks, A. B. (1995). The New German Party Finance Law. *German Politics*, 4, 101–121.

Pelizzo, R. (2004). From Principle to Practice. Constitutional Principles and the Transformation of Party Finance in Germany and Italy. *Comparative European Politics*, 2(2), 123–141.

Pelizzo, R., and F. Stapenhurst. (2012). *Parliamentary Oversight Tools*. London: Routledge.

Pinto-Duschinsky, M. (2002). Financing Politics: A Global View. *Journal of Democracy*, 13(4), 59–86.

Poguntke, T. (1994). Parties in a Legalistic Culture: The Case of Germany. In Richard S. Katz and Peter Mair (Eds.) *How Parties Organize*, pp. 185–215. London: SAGE Publications.

Pujas, V. (2000). Finanziamento dei partiti e controllo dei mezzi di comunicazione. In Mark Gilbert and Gianfranco Pasquino (Eds.) *Politica in Italia. Edizione 2000* pp. 149–164. Bologna: il Mulino.

Pujas, V., and M. Rhodes (1999). Party Finance and Political Scandal in Italy, Spain and France. *West European Politics*, 3, 41–63.

Pulzer, P. (2001). Votes and Resources: Political Finance in Germany. *German Politics and Society*, 19(1), 1–36.

Scarrow, S. (2006). Beyond the Scandals? *German Politics*, 15(4), 376–392.

Stapenhurst, R. (2011). *Legislative Oversight and Corruption: Presidentialism and Parliamentarianism Revisited*. Unpublished PhD thesis. Australian National University.

8   Conclusions

Corruption in government is complex and constantly changing, draining national and international resources, affecting society, and attracting ever-more media and public concern. The need to reduce it represents a constant challenge to the institutions tasked with developing anti-corruption programs. Over the past decade or so, it has been increasingly recognized that political institutions are important when it comes to curbing corruption. Further, research has shown that legislatures in parliamentary systems are more effective at controlling corruption than are the legislatures in presidential systems. Until recently, however, there has been relatively little attention paid to understanding the mechanics of how legislative oversight actually helps to reduce corruption.

In this book we confirm previous work that shows that the type of government system (semi-presidential, presidential, or parliamentary) is a determining factor in the effectiveness of addressing corruption. By examining semi-presidential as well as presidential and parliamentary systems, we have demonstrated that the availability of oversight tools to a legislature is a major factor in the latter's success at helping to curb corruption. We also considered how the core functions of a legislature—oversight, legislation/policy-making, and representation—are each able to contribute to the control of corruption. However, we also explored how and why legislatures may themselves be part of the problem of corruption as well as part of the solution.

In Chapter 2 we examined the phenomenon of corruption and its definition, costs, and consequences, along with a consideration of multi-stakeholder strategies to curb corruption. In Chapters 3 and 4 we looked at legislatures as part of the solution to corruption. The former chapter examined how the core functions of parliament—oversight, legislative/policy-making, and representation—can be used by legislatures as they participate in multi-stakeholder networks and coalitions against corruption, while the latter presented an in-depth comparative study of how legislatures in Ghana and Nigeria carry out these functions. Building on the comparative case study, in Chapter 5 we explored the relationship between social trust/confidence in parliament and the political will to curb corruption. In Chapters 6 and 7 we looked specifically at legislative corruption and considered various mechanisms, such as codes of conduct, electoral laws, and campaign financing, which can be used to reduce such corruption. Here, we summarize the main issues considered in each of these chapters and present key recommendations stemming from our analyses for enhancing the role of legislatures in curbing corruption.

CORRUPTION—DEFINITION, COSTS, AND CONSEQUENCES

We examined in Chapter 2 the phenomenon of corruption and its definition, costs, and consequences, as well as giving consideration to multi-stakeholder strategies for curbing corruption. We noted—as expounded by Jain (2001)—that three basic forms of corruption exist; for ease of reference we reprise in Figure 3.1 from Chapter 3 in Figure 8.1. The first of these forms, bureaucratic corruption, is principally connected with the perversion of implementing laws while, in its most crude form, it involves civil servants taking backhands. The second form of corruption is grand corruption, defined by Jain (2001, p. 105) as occurring when politicians ". . . [have] worked out an equilibrium relationship [with their] constituents and [are] able to make and implement economic and political decisions" and is intended to serve their own interests, often to the detriment of the citizens that they in theory represent. Finally, there is electoral corruption (a subcategory of grand corruption), which is the form of corruption that we have been mostly concerned with in this

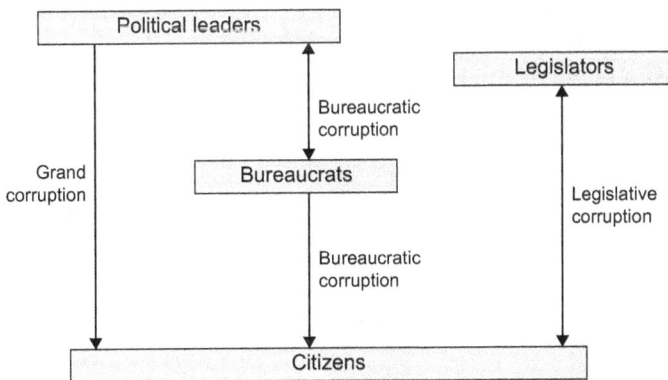

Figure 8.1 Types of Corruption

Source: Jain (2001).

book. Electoral corruption occurs when political candidates are involved in either accepting or actively sourcing campaign contributions and in so doing undermine the political financing laws in place. Electoral corruption can range from passive forms—either serendipitously accepting a generous contribution from a banned source or accepting amounts in excess of the limits in place—to more active forms, such as buying votes. A number of institutional solutions have been developed over the years to combat electoral corruption, including anti-corruption agencies, electoral commissions, and the implementation of legislative and normative dispositions. In addition, parliamentary committees have been convened to provide surveillance and to endeavor to keep incidences of electoral corruption to a minimum.

Strategies to Curb Corruption

While there is broad agreement on the forms that corruption may take—bureaucratic, grand, or electoral—and an appreciation of the economic and societal costs involved, the central role that legislatures can perform through their core functions of legislation/policy-making, representation, and oversight in relation to deterring and combatting corruption tends not to be fully understood or well leveraged in anti-corruption initiatives. Consequently, although most anti-corruption frameworks may reference the importance of legislative oversight, supreme audit institutions, public hearings of draft laws, and freedom of information, they almost invariably fail to properly appreciate or take account of how these different elements should be "knitted" together into a coherent strategy. Figure 1.1 in Chapter 1, reprised here as Figure 8.2 for ease of reference, shows by way of example an anti-corruption strategic framework proposed by the World Bank.[1] As we concluded in Chapter 2, what is overlooked in this and other models is the essential central role that an effective legislature can play in (1) enforcing institutional restraints on power through collaboration with the supreme audit institution; (2) encouraging civil society participation through draft-law scrutiny in the public hearings of legislative committees; (3) engendering political accountability as the result of passing political competition and campaign finance legislation; and (4) developing codes of conduct and ethics regimes for members of the executive, legislature, and bureaucracy. In particular, we made a strong case that, given that combatting a complex problem such as corruption requires a strategy that is both multidimensional and allows for a multi-stakeholder approach, the legislature should be seen as a principal plank in any framework designed for curbing corruption.

Having overviewed the overall strategies for curbing corruption at the state level, we next moved on to looking in greater detail at the role played by legislatures when it comes to tackling corruption.

Political accountability
- Political competition
- Transparency in party financing
- Asset declarations,
  conflict of interest rules
- *Freedom of information*
- Investigative journalism

Institutional restraints on power
- Independent and effective judiciary
- Independent prosecution,
  enforcement
- *Legislative oversight**
- *Supreme audit institution*

Competitive private sector
- Economic policy reform
- Competitive restructuring of
  monopolies
- Regulatory
  quality/simplification
- Transparency in corporate
  governance
- Collective business associations

**Civil society
participation**
- *Public hearings of
  draft laws*
- Citizen oversight
- Role for NGOs

Anti-corruption

Public sector management
- Meritocratic civil service with adequate pay
- Budget management (coverage, treasury,
  procurement, audit)
- Tax and customs
- Sectoral service delivery (health, education, energy)
- Decentralization with accountability

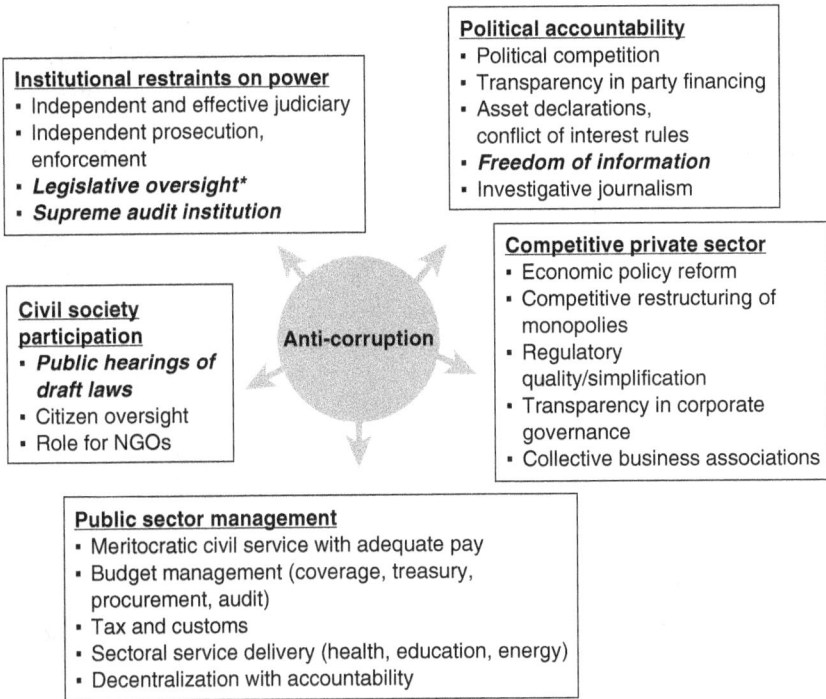

Figure 8.2 A Multifaceted Anti-corruption Strategy
NGO = nongovernmental organization.

*Mechanisms in italic refer to legislative oversight tools.
Source: Adapted from Kaufmann and Dininio (2006)

THE ROLE OF LEGISLATURES

Part of the Solution

Chapter 3 analyzed the relative importance of the different mandated functions of legislatures as parts of the solution to corruption, and Chapter 4 fol-
lowed with a side-by-side comparison of legislatures in Ghana and Nigeria
in terms of how they each carry out these functions. To begin, we highlighted
the fact that accountability is vital and that lower levels of corruption are
seen to correlate with political systems in which officials are fully accountable for their expenses. Clarifying the role of the legislature as the people's
overseer of the executive, we next proceeded to examine how each of the
three core functions of parliament—oversight, legislative/policy-making
and representation—figure in multi-stakeholder networks and coalitions
against corruption. Interestingly, we saw how technological developments

are increasingly providing citizens with new and effective ways to voice their concerns on public issues, and in the process are causing a subtle but definite diminution of the parliamentary representative function. Furthermore, we saw that with the major part of legislation increasingly being initiated by the executive branch of government, the importance of the legislature's legislative function is also tending to erode in most contemporary political systems. Reduced influence in both the representative and legislative functions of parliaments has automatically coincided, however, with an increase in the importance of the oversight role. Importantly, it is clear that when legislatures are effective in performing their oversight function, they make a significant contribution to both detecting and preventing corruption, and in turn this makes a significant contribution to the overall legitimacy of the parliament as an institution and to the legitimacy of the political system as a whole. For this reason, oversight of policy and budget implementation is now generally seen as the single most important function that a legislature can perform.

Part of the Problem

As was discussed in Chapter 2, Lederman, Loayza, and Soares (2005) points to presidential forms of government being generally more prone to corruption than parliamentary systems, stating that ". . . parliamentary systems [along with democracy, political stability, and freedom of the press] . . . are associated with lower corruption" (Lederman, Loayza, and Soares, 2005, p. 28) and reasoning that ". . . political macrostructure determine[s] the incentives for those in office to be honest and police and punish [the] misbehaviour of people inside and outside the government bureaucracy" (Lederman, Loayza, and Soares, 2005, p. 37). Our own analysis both confirmed and goes further than Lederman et al.'s finding to produce a first important conclusion: that meso-level institutions (such as legislative committees, codes of conduct and supreme audit institutions) are more determinative in levels of corruption than are macrostructures; that is, whether a system is presidential or parliamentary. Internal and external oversight tools (the meso-level institutions), facilitating conditions such as the size of parliamentary libraries, number of research staff, and the socio-political context in which the legislature operates, are all determinative in the legislature's ability to curb corruption.

The next lesson we were able to learn is that legislatures can play a key pivotal role in curbing corruption by performing their oversight function. Or, to articulate the same idea in a slightly different way, when legislatures are effective in performing their oversight function, they make a significant contribution to both preventing and detecting corruption. Unpicking the relationship between oversight effectiveness, political willingness to curb corruption, and legitimacy was an important part of the discussion. We saw that different legislative oversight tools come into play to combat different types of corruption—although to different extents—just as the facilitating factors, such as trust in the legislature, shape the environment in which the legislature operates. Significantly, we singled out the willingness of the legislature to perform its functions of oversight to its full capacity and ability. In fact, the ability and willingness of parliaments to tackle corruption is a major contributor to the effectiveness with which the oversight function is performed and makes a significant contribution to the legitimacy of the parliament as an institution as well as to the legitimacy of the political system as a whole.

PUBLIC TRUST AND POLITICAL WILL

In Chapter 5 we explored the relationship between social trust/confidence in parliament and the political will to curb corruption. As the body made up of elected representatives of civil society, legislatures should in theory command public confidence and be free of illegal behavior, but the unhappy reality is that corruption and malpractice has been exposed in many, if not most, parliaments across the world. Jain (2001, p. 75) highlighted the issue of legislative corruption, defining it as ". . . the manner and the extent to which the voting behavior of legislators can be influenced. Legislators can be bribed by interest groups to enact legislation that [favors their clients/ members]. This type of corruption . . . include[s] vote-buying, whether by legislators in their attempts to get re-elected or by officials in the executive branch in their efforts to have some legislation enacted." The presence of such corruption (perceived and actual) in parliaments along with other illicit and unethical practices is not surprisingly a major turn-off for citizens. In fact, global surveys show public trust in parliament to be at a lamentably low level, with legislatures enjoying very little public confidence relative to other institutions. Indeed, Figure 8.3, reprising previously presented data, represents the aggregation of public opinion data from 100 countries

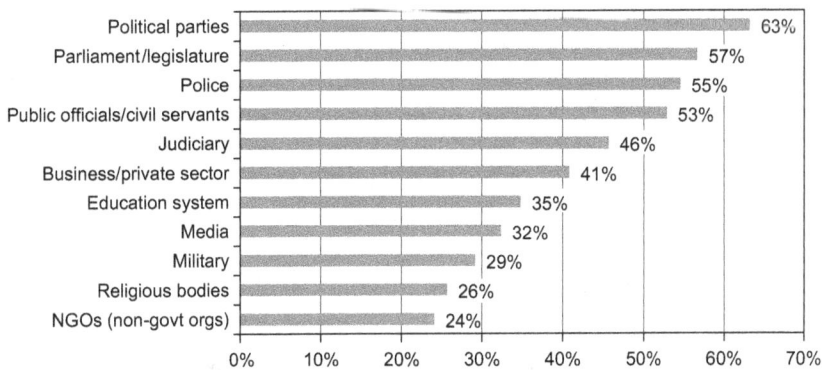

Figure 8.3 Percentage of Respondents Viewing Public Institutions as Corrupt (n = 100)
NGO = nongovernmental organization.
Source: Transparency International, Corruption Barometer.

around the world, and shows how, almost universally, citizens regard their legislatures as the second-most corrupt institutions after political parties. The conclusion to be drawn is very clear: citizens across the globe have very little trust in their parliaments. Furthermore, as we show in this book, there seems to be a very high correspondence between the percentage of survey respondents who have little or no trust in parliaments and those who think that parliaments are corrupt. The real and perceived presence of corruption, illicit and other unethical practices in parliaments, and a general lack of public trust in legislatures inevitably represent barriers to achieving effective anti-corruption surveillance of the executive by parliament. For this reason, in addition to ensuring that the legislature is properly resourced to perform its oversight function from a capacity standpoint, it is necessary for regulations to be in place that are effective at eliminating electoral corruption, fraud, and unethical behavior within the legislature itself.

Regaining Public Trust: Codes of Ethics and Codes of Conduct

As the level of public trust in parliaments has dropped, it is clear that legislatures no longer have the level of legitimacy that they once enjoyed. Parliaments are, along with political parties, the least-trusted political institutions in the world. This amounts to what many regard as a serious governance crisis. As corruption and other forms of unethical behavior are believed to be the cause of the loss of trust in and legitimacy of parliaments, many have in recent times implemented ethics reforms in order to regain their legitimacy. In Chapter 6 we discussed some of the specific steps that have been taken by parliaments to promote good conduct within the legislative arena. Thus, for example, parliaments have adopted codes of ethics and codes of conduct, they have introduced dispositions concerning the disclosure and the registration of interests, and they have in several cases set up ethics committees in parliament. Codes of conduct are more detailed sets of dispositions that can be adopted for regulating the behavior of parliamentarians in the legislative arena, are not aspirational, and establish clear sanctions for violations of the norms that they set for parliamentarians. But while these dispositions regulate the behavior of members after they are elected, and are meant to prevent instances of corrupt and unethical behavior inside parliament, they do very little for preventing the election of corrupt candidates or for preventing, minimizing, or eradicating electoral corruption.

Cleaning up the Electoral Process

Finally, in Chapter 7 we looked at how, following a series of corruption scandals in the early 21st century, in order to regulate the behavior of politicians in the electoral arena and consequently curb electoral corruption, parliaments have needed to adopt normative and legal dispositions, including electoral legislation (electoral laws, electoral codes, etc.) and rules governing party and campaign finance. These regulations cover four distinct areas. Some of these dispositions place bans and limitations on the sources and the amounts of funds that parties and candidates can receive; some dispositions concern public funding, financial subsidies, and subsidies in kind to both political parties and electoral candidates; some dispositions are intended to regulate the level of spending; while a fourth set of dispositions concerns the report mechanisms, the oversight of campaign finance, and the sanctions that can be applied for violations of campaign legislation.

Since it is generally believed that the single most important determinant of electoral corruption is the cost of campaigning, some dispositions have been introduced that place limits on how much money parties and candidates may spend in the course of one election, and provide parties and candidates with public subsidies and free or inexpensive broadcasting. In other instances, limits have been placed on the amount of private and corporate funds that parties and candidates are allowed to accept. Campaign regulations have introduced in various jurisdictions strict norms, monitoring bodies, and sanctions for violations. We concluded that, based on data from International IDEA, regulations were substantially more prolific than a decade ago, particularly for regulating party finance, and that the number of countries where parties receive public contributions to reduce the need for resorting to corruption has increased. We went on to put forward the idea that this is an area that needs to be better regulated, and further surmised that there is a need for legislators to work toward reducing the cost of politics as opposed to prioritizing finding ways to provide more funding.

CONCLUSIONS AND RECOMMENDATIONS

For several years, scholars and practitioners have viewed parliaments as the representatives of society and as the institutional bodies that have the constitutional task of overseeing the executive. The international community has generally regarded legislative oversight as the appropriate institutional mechanism to ensure that executives are kept accountable for their actions, their expenditures, and their policy implementation. Further, the international community has generally believed that the creation of a system of accountability in which executives explain and account to other institutions, to the citizens, and to various civil society groups could play a key role in curbing corruption.

Over the past decade, various studies have shown that effective oversight contributes to improving the quality, the functioning, the performance, and the legitimacy of a democratic regime (Pelizzo and Stapenhurst, 2012). They have also shown that effective oversight makes a significant contribution toward curbing corruption (Pelizzo and Stapenhurst, 2012), improving good governance (Stapenhurst, Pelizzo, and Jacobs, 2013), securing the conditions for a more equitable distribution of resources (Pelizzo, 2012), ensuring higher rates of growth and development, and making democracy work better (Pelizzo and Stapenhurst, 2012).

Initially, it was believed that oversight effectiveness could be equated to the oversight capacity, to the number of oversight tools at the disposal of a legislature (Pelizzo and Stapenhurst, 2004), to the powers and the oversight mandate of a legislature, and to the context within which a legislature operates (for a review of the literature, see Stapenhurst, 2011). In other words, all of these studies focused on static, structural, and mechanic conditions. In a second wave of studies the static, structural, and mechanic approach to the study of legislative oversight was complemented and integrated by what we could call, for lack of a better term, a dynamic approach to the study of oversight. Stapenhurst (2011) made clear that the effectiveness with which legislatures perform their oversight function reflects not only the powers and the tools at their disposal but also the level of support, trust, and confidence that they enjoy.

Building on this work, we have shown in this book and its companion volume (Pelizzo and Stapenhurst, 2013) that voter trust is important for ensuring that legislative oversight activities are carried out effectively, because if legislatures lack the support of the population they may not have the strength, the legitimacy, and the will to engage seriously in their oversight tasks.

The mirror image of this is, of course, that popular perception views legislatures as part of the problem—we have shown that there is a strong correlation between people's trust in parliament and perceived corruption.

The key contribution this book makes (and Pelizzo and Stapenhurst, 2012) is underlining the importance of political will for ensuring effective oversight and fighting corruption, regardless of whether the focus is on the role of the legislature in reducing executive and bureaucratic corruption or on the legislature taking responsibility for the reduction, curbing legislative corruption.

Recommendations

Improving the Role of Legislatures as Part of the Solution to Corruption

The incentives for office holders are largely shaped by meso-level institutions such as internal and external oversight tools, factors that support the oversight function, and contextual factors such as the form of government and public trust in parliament.

However, our analysis suggests that the importance of oversight tools is less than originally thought, is conditional, and varies across forms of government. Not all oversight tools are equally effective, and what works for some forms of government may not work well, or at all, in other systems. Hence, the "one size fits all" approach is inadequate when it comes to strengthening legislative capacity and curbing corruption. It is critical that legislatures adopt a systems approach to oversight, choosing the tools and mechanisms that will work best in their system and not looking for some good practice at the global level. More important, it is the willingness of legislators to use effectively the oversight tools at their disposal rather than increase the number of tools, that makes legislative oversight effective. If politicians lack the political will to oversee government effectively, and thereby help curb corruption, then any number of tools and mechanisms will be useless.

Moreover, facilitating conditions, such as the size of legislative libraries and the number of parliamentary research staff, are important, as are factors such as trust in parliament, which shape the environment within which legislatures operate.

Improving Public Trust and Confidence in Legislatures

Legislatures are among the least-trusted of public institutions. This undermines the effectiveness of parliaments in many ways, not least in their ability to oversee governments and help curb corruption. While political will and trust are important for fighting corruption at the executive level, corruption at the legislative level prevents legislatures from adequately performing their oversight tasks and fighting corruption. This is the reason why, if legislatures are to fight corruption, they must first rid themselves of corruption.

In order to regain the confidence of the citizens, parliaments have taken several steps: they have adopted codes of ethics and codes of conduct, they have introduced dispositions concerning the disclosure and the registration of interests, and they have in several cases set up ethics committees in parliament. Such regimes, when effectively implemented, can help respond to legitimacy crises.

Furthermore, while it is clear that regulations concerning party finances are more common than they were a decade ago, much remains to be done in the area of political and campaign finance. For instance, legislators and institutional reformers should focus on reducing the cost of politics rather than on providing more generous funding. This could be done by, for example, providing free political broadcasts and subsidies-in-kind, while at the same time placing stricter limits on how much political parties and candidates can spend, especially during elections. Here again, it appears that formal mechanisms are insufficient. The political will to oversee political finance is essential to ensure that political finance is overseen effectively.

NOTE

1. Transparency International proposes a similar multifaceted strategy, using the notion of "pillars of integrity," where one such pillar is legislative oversight.

REFERENCES

Jain, A. K. (2001). *Political Economy of Corruption.* London: Routledge.

Kaufmann, D., and P. Dininio. (2006). Corruption: A Key Challenge for Development. In R. Stapenhurst, N. Johnston, and R. Pelizzo (Eds.) *The Role of Parliament in Curbing Corruption,* pp. 13–24. Washington, DC: World Bank.

Lederman, D., N. Loayza, and R. R. Soares. (2005). Accountability and Corruption: Political Institutions Matter. *Economics and Politics,* 17(1), 1–35.

Pelizzo, R. (2012). *Le strategie della crescita: Saggi di politica economica.* Napoli: Guida.

Pelizzo, R., and R. Stapenhurst. (2004). *Tools for Legislative Oversight: An Empirical Investigation.* World Bank Policy Research Working Paper No. 3388.

Pelizzo, R., and R. Stapenhurst. (2012). *Parliamentary Oversight Tools.* London: Routledge.

Pelizzo, R., and R. Stapenhurst. (2013). "Government Accountability and Legislative Oversight." London: Routledge.

Stapenhurst, F. (2011). *Legislative Oversight and Curbing Corruption: Presidentialism and Parliamentarianism Revisited.* Unpublished PhD thesis. Canberra: Australian National University.

Stapenhurst, F., R. Pelizzo, and K. Jacobs. (2013). *Follow the Money: A Global Study of PACs.* London: Pluto Press.

Transparency International Corruption Barometer: www.transparency.org/gcb/2013.

Expert Monograph: Putting a Stop to the Laundering of Corrupt Money[1]

Corrupt leaders will make every effort to disguise their ill-gotten gains by portraying the amounts illegally gained as though they are derived from a legitimate source, by inserting them into economic circulation—typically by transferring the funds across international borders, using various disguised layering techniques, into legitimate financial institutions. Not all corrupt money is laundered "offshore," however. For example, in some countries, corrupt cash is used domestically to buy votes and other favors.

Whatever the method or process used to attempt to launder corrupt money, inserting roadblocks to prevent this from happening is a key element in any anti-corruption strategy. Deterrents are essential to discourage corrupt activities and cause corrupt leaders to pause and think before acting. If they are unable to launder their proceeds, how will they ever be able to use their new-found assets? Is it worth the risk if they cannot derive benefit from these illegal activities?

An effective national and international anti-money laundering regime should be part of a two-pronged approach to address the scourge of corruption. First, tackle corruption, and in a parallel way fight the laundering of corrupt money. Parliamentarians have a critical role to play in both of these processes.

Let me make a couple of distinctions early in this piece. While parliamentarians should be concerned about petty bribery (e.g., the payment of $50 to "facilitate" the approval of a permit of some sort), their impact will be biggest if they challenge the problem of "big ticket" or the "grand larceny" type of corruption. By this I mean the billions that are stolen, and have been stolen, by leaders. For example see Table A.1. There are also large amounts of money laundered through the United Kingdom (U.K.) each year—estimated to be £48 billion (2% of the U.K.'s GDP)[2] And let's not forget the billions embezzled by some of the more contemporary leaders like Libya's Muammar al-Gaddafi and Egypt's Hosni Mubarak. How many schools, hospitals, immunizations, and miles of roads could have been put into place if these billions had not been lost to corruption?

Table A.1   Money Stolen by Leaders[1]

Leader	Country	Dollars (in billions)
Former president Suharto	Indonesia	$15–$35
Former president Ferdinand Marcos	Philippines	$5–$10
Former president Mabuto Sese Seko	Zaire	$5

[1] These figures were reported in Transparency International's 2004 Global Corruption Report. http://issuu.com/transparencyinternational/docs/2004_gcr_politicalcorruption_en?e=2496456/2106435

Distinction number two—An effective anti-money laundering regime is the preventative measure to stop or curtail the laundering of corrupt money. Despite these best efforts, however, corrupt money will "slip between the cracks" and find its way into offshore or domestic bank accounts. As Raymond Baker, Director of Global Financial Integrity, asserts—"Indeed, global corruption has not diminished despite ten years of effort. Assets now stashed in tax havens around the globe are estimated at $11.5 trillion, and non-bank cash deposits outside the country of origin are rising" (Global Financial Integrity, 2013). The recovery and repatriation of stolen assets is the "treatment" side of this equation whereby governments and parliamentarians launch efforts to locate the stolen corrupt assets and return them to their rightful owners—their citizens. The Stolen Asset Recovery Initiative (StAR)—a joint project of the World Bank and the United Nations Office on Drugs and Crime (UNODC)—is an excellent source of information and support to parliamentarians as they embark upon this quest.

The fact that corruption and money laundering are clandestine activities inhibits accurate and complete estimates of the full quantum and level of this type of activity. Given that qualification, however, a 2007 study by KPMG concluded that US$ 1 trillion per year, including corrupt money, is being laundered every year. As Baker estimates, since 1948 India has lost over $460 billion in illicit financial flows—mostly from corruption.[3] (Global Financial Integrity, 2010). WikiLeaks recently revealed, via U.S. diplomatic cables, that bribery in Russia approximates $300 billion per year (BBC News, 2010). And the list goes on. Suffice it to say that the problem is a huge one, and it does not appear to be going away.

This is where Parliamentarians enter the scene. Too often legislators underestimate the important role they can play in demanding the transparency and accountability of the executive branch of government. While it is understood that partisan politics and party discipline are realities of life, this does not preclude an active and assertive legislature. Presidents, Prime Ministers, and Cabinet Ministers should not be free to pilfer government coffers and rob citizens of their inalienable right to move out of the ranks of the poor. Corruption leads to a gross misallocation of national resources and an increase in income and asset disparities that defy justification.

Parliamentarians' important role in combating corruption and money laundering can be achieved in a number of different ways:

- Through debates and questions in the legislature itself;
- Through the work of an auditor general, or equivalent, that reports directly to parliament; and
- By enquiry and investigative work by a public accounts committee of parliament.

An effective anti-money laundering regime acts as a significant deterrent to corruption. While money laundering and anti-money laundering (AML) are somewhat technical, GOPAC has de-mystified the topic by publishing the *Anti-Money Laundering Action Guide for Parliamentarians* in GOPAC's three official languages—English, French, and Spanish (GOPAC, 2012). The Action Guide can be downloaded from GOPAC's website at www.gopacnetwork.org. In this document, the size, scale, and scope of money laundering is described; a brief overview of the modus operandi of corrupt money launderers is provided; some of the jargon and language of money laundering is highlighted, and a variety of tools that parliamentarians can use in this fight are featured.

The first item in the parliamentarians' tool kit is an assessment of the quality and extent of the anti-money laundering regime in his/her country. This information can be gleaned from a variety of sources:

If the jurisdiction in question is a signatory to the United Nations Convention Against Corruption (UNCAC),[4] there are various provisions of this Convention relating to money laundering that the country should be complying with. The applicable sections of the UNCAC are:

Article 14: Measures to prevent money laundering
Article 23: Laundering of proceeds of crime
Article 53: Measures for direct recovery of property
Article 54: Mechanisms for recovery of property through international cooperation in confiscation
Article 57: Return and disposal of assets
Article 58: Financial Intelligence Unit

In the context of these UNCAC articles, here are some good questions for parliamentarians to ask:

On legislative provisions and practices:
- Is there legislation in place in your country for the prevention and detection of money laundering, including requirements of effective customer identification (Know Your Customer), record-keeping and reporting of suspicious transactions by financial institutions? Is the legislation comprehensive?

- Has a financial intelligence unit (FIU)[5] been established to serve as a national centre for the collection, analysis and dissemination of information regarding potential money-laundering?
- Does the FIU report to Parliament and respond to recommendations?
- Is Parliament engaged in the budgetary allocation for the FIU?
- Have any money laundering cases been prosecuted?
- Have any corrupt assets been recovered?

GOPAC, in partnership with UNDP, has developed an effective survey instrument, the "Anti-Corruption Assessment Tool for Parliamentarians," which can be used by parliamentarians to assess how well their jurisdiction is doing in the fight against corruption and money laundering. It uses the United Nations Convention Against Corruption (UNCAC) as the benchmark.[6]

Parliamentarians can also access reports emanating from the Financial Action Task Force (FATF), the global standard-setting body for anti-money laundering, including peer reviews of member countries, mutual evaluation reports, and lists of high-risk and non-cooperative jurisdictions. These documents may highlight deficiencies in the country's anti-money laundering regime.

The FATF is also represented by Eight FATF Style Regional Bodies (FSRBs) around the world. These local organizations can be a very useful resource for parliamentarians seeking specific information about the strengths and weaknesses of their own country's anti-money laundering efforts.[7]

The Organization for Economic Co-operation and Development (OECD) provides regular updates about the state of anti-money laundering efforts and may point to shortfalls in individual countries.

For those countries where there is no anti-money laundering regime in place, template legislation developed by the UNODC/IMF and the Commonwealth Secretariat is available for both common law and civil law countries.[8] The model laws incorporate the requirements contained in international instruments and the FATF 40+9 Recommendations in particular, and strengthen or supplement them in light of the actual practice of a number of countries (Financial Action Task Force, 2001). Naturally, these laws serve as models only, and legislators need to customize these laws to fit within their own customs and conventions; nonetheless, they are an excellent place to start.

If the country has anti-money laundering legislation, but upon examination parliamentarians ascertain that there are weaknesses in the existing laws, amendments can be tabled in their legislature. Government members, and opposition members for that matter, can, in the first instance, try to convince the government of the day that changes are needed. Should this not produce results, Parliamentarians are able, in addition to tabling amendments, to put questions to the government in the legislature, and/or engage the media and civil society in the fight for improvements. It is also sometimes the case that anti-money laundering is in place, but cannot be effectively implemented because a financial intelligence unit (FIU) has not been established or adequately mandated and resourced.

The establishment of an effective FIU is critical for success in a country's anti-money laundering efforts. Good legislation alone will not suffice. The World Bank and the IMF describe an FIU as a central national agency responsible for receiving, analyzing, and transmitting disclosures on suspicious transactions to the competent authorities (The World Bank, 2004).

THE ROLE OF PARLIAMENTARIANS IN THE ESTABLISHMENT OF AN FIU

Parliamentarians have an important role to play in the development, launching, and monitoring of an FIU as follows: advising on how to structure the anti-money laundering organization; ensuring that the model is adequately mandated and resourced and built according to international (FATF) standards; and finally, creating, and reporting on, their own success stories. Each of these issues will be covered in detail below.

Parliamentarians play a valuable role through providing advice and comment on the *design and organization* of the FIU. There are various models that have been adopted by countries depending on the country's size, political culture, public policy traditions, privacy laws, and its overall legal framework. For example, FIUs can be structured as part of the administrative, law enforcement, or judicial arms of the government, and report notionally to a Minister of Finance, or a Minister of Justice. In either case, politics and partisanship must be avoided at all costs and therefore the reporting lines in these cases must be oversight only—with no involvement in day-to-day operations. Alternatively in some jurisdictions the FIU reports to the head of a central bank or a law enforcement agency. Whatever structure is adopted, the independence and integrity of the FIU is paramount to avoid jeopardizing or compromising ongoing investigations.

Parliamentarians can also ensure that the FIU is properly *mandated and resourced*. In this regard, it should be noted that technical assistance to establish and strengthen FIUs is available from a number of organizations, including the World Bank, the International Monetary Fund (IMF), the FATF, GOPAC, and others. How many staff members and the budget an FIU will need to operate effectively and efficiently are difficult questions to answer because there are many variables at play.

Parliamentarians can ask researchers to benchmark other comparable jurisdictions that have successfully launched an FIU. By way of comparison only, Canada's FIU—the Financial Transactions and Reports Analysis Centre of Canada (FINTRAC)—has an annual budget of approximately $55 million and a headcount of about 350 people.[9] FINTRAC has a reputation for being a solid FIU that functions very well.[10] Keep in mind, however, that a smaller agency may suffice, in particular to get started. To put this budget in context, Canada is the eleventh largest economy in the world with a GDP approaching $2 trillion annually, and a relatively small population of some 34 million people spread across a huge area (OECD, 2012). The FIU in Thailand has an annual budget of 178,942,100 Baht (US$ 6,100,000) and it employs 226 people—in a country with a population of 66.7 million people, and a GDP of US$ 377.2 (Anti-Money Laudering Office of Thailand, 2011). The resources needed for an FIU need to be carefully examined in the context of each individual country's circumstances; but, regardless, parliamentarians should be engaged in the budgetary allocation to the FIU.

For international guidance, the *Egmont Group* of Financial Intelligence Units is an international network of FIUs designed to exchange information to follow the suspected proceeds of crime and to foster the implementation of domestic anti-money laundering programs. In 2012, the EGMONT Group comprised 131 members—the vast majority of global FIUs. To meet the standards of Egmont membership, an FIU must be a centralized unit within a nation or jurisdiction committed to detect criminal financial activity and ensure adherence to laws against financial crimes, including money laundering. The Egmont Group is the world leader in this area, and they apply a rigorous level of due diligence before new members are admitted. Parliamentarians should be asking whether or not their FIU is a member of the Egmont Group and if not, why not.

Parliamentarians can strive to create their own success story. For example, the admission of the Kyrgyz Republic Financial Intelligence Unit into the Egmont Group in 2009 was a rewarding experience for GOPAC and for parliamentarians from the Kyrgyz Republic. The reason is that some years ago the GOPAC anti-money laundering team worked with parliamentarians from that country and assisted them in drafting and successfully introducing anti-money laundering legislation into their parliament.

Parliamentarians made this happen—so it can be done! In 2012 GOPAC's national chapter in the Philippines drove through significant amendments to the country's anti-money laundering laws. As a result of these legislative changes, the Financial Action Task Force (FATF) upgraded the Philippine's status and acknowledged that the country is making "sufficient progress" in meeting international standards for fighting money laundering. This is another example of parliamentarians taking the initiative.

One of the ongoing challenges is the demonstration of positive results from the country's anti-money laundering regime, especially the FIU. The question is often asked, and should be asked—how many successful prosecutions of money launderers have there been as a result of analytical work done by the national FIU? Legislators should be asking this question to ensure that value-for-money is being obtained. After all, the work done by the FIU costs taxpayer's money and diverts scarce national resources from other priorities. The linkage between FIU analysis and anti-money laundering prosecutions is often a tenuous one, and often difficult to prove. A useful

hint—at the launch of the FIU, or later, build into the reporting and evaluation mechanisms of the FIU a way to correlate, to the extent possible, the
relationship between FIU work and prosecutions.

In addition to evaluating the quality and performance of their country's
anti-money regime, and its associated FIU, parliamentarians can intervene
on a variety of policy and legislative issues.

A key component of an anti-money laundering regime is the criminalization of money laundering.

It is very important to note that the criminalisation of money laundering must be both directed to the jurisdiction where the corrupt money
originates—and, equally importantly, to the jurisdiction in receipt of
the corrupt funds. The criminalization of money laundering should
cover predicate offences committed in other countries as if the predicate
offence occurred domestically. *Anti-Money Laundering* (AML) tools
should be used to seize and confiscate stolen assets even if the predicate
offence has been committed abroad. Often, countries do not succeed
in effectively pursuing the proceeds of foreign predicate offences; however, that is usually because jurisdictions require proof of the predicate
offence. Parliamentarians need to be aware that such a threshold is not
in line with FATF requirements. Money laundering is often described as
cash being placed in the financial system, or cash being converted into
assets. This can leave the impression that law enforcement authorities
only have a short window of opportunity to detect money laundering—
i.e. during the conversion, placement or concealment stages. However,
the required criminalisation of money laundering should cover cash and
any other property that is directly or indirectly connected to the crime.
The FATF also requires that jurisdictions need to be able to seize, freeze
and confiscate all property that is the proceeds of crime and all property
that is used as an instrumentality in a crime. Parliamentarians should
rest assured that the requirements of the FATF in relation to the criminalisation of money laundering are fully in line with UN Conventions
(e.g. Vienna and Palermo) (GOPAC Anti-Money Laundering Action
Guide, 2011, pp. 35–36).

A country's anti-money laundering laws and procedures should include
enhanced monitoring and due diligence associated with the financial transactions of *Politically Exposed Persons (PEPs)*. Politically Exposed Persons
are defined in the UNCAC as individuals, their family members, and asso-
ciates who are, or have been, entrusted with prominent public functions.
While this topic is a sensitive one because it implicates the very same parliamentarians who are fighting for tougher regimes—laws and regulations
should make no distinction between domestic and foreign PEPs. These individuals are those who, because of their role in the public sector, are exposed
to bribes and the temptation to launder the proceeds of their crimes. Senior

management of financial institutions and intermediaries should annually review the PEPs list and their transactions for the year and complete a report to document the same. It should also be an established policy that time limits are not established for PEPs after they relinquish their role as public officers.

One aspect closely linked to the matter of Politically Exposed Persons is the requirement for public officials to annually, and at the beginning and end of a mandate and perhaps beyond, disclose their assets and income. Financial and business interest information that would be publically disclosed would include real estate, vehicles, art, jewelry, financial investments and liabilities, stock holdings, other income sources, gifts received, and positions held outside public office. This matter is dealt with more fully *in GOPAC's Handbook on Parliamentary Ethics and Conduct*, but suffice it to say for our purposes here that transparency of these assets and income sheds further light on the activities and conduct of PEPs (GOPAC, n.d.).

To comply with FATF standards, financial institutions globally are adopting stringent due diligence and "know your customer" (KYC) procedures and techniques. *Know Your Customer* includes client identification requirements and the verification of the source of funds for accounts. As a result of this enhanced scrutiny, money launderers have resorted to more sophisticated techniques to hide the true source of funds. This includes an array of methods, including layering the transactions through a series of shelf corporations with nominee directors. Establishing the identity of the beneficial owner(s) of the funds is often a very challenging task. When one combines this with the fact that financial institutions and intermediaries—despite perhaps their best intentions—have an inherent conflict-of-interest because they are anxious to accept large deposits from a business perspective, the challenge becomes an even more daunting one. Banks assert, with some legitimacy, that it is sometimes next to impossible to unravel all the complex layers that corrupt money launderers put in their way. Why not then, reverse the onus and place the burden of proof on the depositors themselves?

The following resolution, which has been adapted from an initiative of Raymond Baker, was adopted unanimously at GOPAC's 5th Global Conference held in Manila, Philippines, in February 2013 at its plenary session:

> . . . the requirement that all financial institutions and intermediaries demand a binding legal declaration of *beneficial ownership* for all deposits and other financial transactions, with sanctions for non-compliance. (GOPAC, 2013)

The intent of this proposal is, wherever possible, to transfer the burden of responsibility of beneficial ownership declaration to depositors with risks associated with false disclosures, including the freezing and confiscation of accounts if this information on beneficial owners proves to be false. While certainly not a panacea—many depositors will still take the risk of false disclosure—it would deter the laundering of some corrupt money, and at the same time spread compliance costs.

An effective anti-money laundering regime is the preventative component in the fight against money laundering and the place where parliamentarians can have a substantial impact. The fact is, however, that some laundered corrupt money escapes detection and finds its way into an account in an offshore or other international financial institution. This may comprise corrupt money laundered abroad before a country instituted an anti-money laundering regime, or funds that have slipped through the net despite that country's best efforts to combat this scourge.

This brings us to the recovery of stolen corrupt assets. How can parliamentarians assist in the orchestration of the repatriation of corrupt assets that are hidden outside the country so that citizens, not corrupt leaders, can benefit from these national assets?

First, beware that this is a very technical and legal minefield that takes much patience and knowledge and, to some extent, is best left to "experts." Parliamentarians, however, can provide much needed motivation, transparency, and oversight as this process develops and evolves.

At a GOPAC/World Bank anti-money laundering workshop in Arusha, Tanzania, in September 2006 a representative from Nigeria's Economic and Financial Crimes Commission described their attempts to recover corrupt money laundered in a banking center in the Caribbean. He had written a letter to the bank in question in the name of the Commission, seeking repatriation of the country's assets. A distant one year later, he received a very polite letter, thanking the representative for his kind letter, and offering their full cooperation—but if, and only if, the Commission would provide the bank with the numbers of specific bank accounts in question! This was more detail than the Commission had access to, but they were very confident corrupt Nigerian official(s) had used this specific bank to launder corrupt money. Unfortunately, they had to give up on their quest for justice given the impossible hurdle set by the bank.

Contrast this with governments who come into power and, for strictly partisan purposes, make unsubstantiated claims of corruption by the outgoing party and begin a "witch hunt" of offshore banks.

What is needed is a balanced approach between the unrealistic requirement by some banks for bank account numbers; and the sublime—unsubstantiated partisan witch hunts conducted by elected officials. A new protocol is needed. Parliamentarians can push for this. GOPAC is working towards conducting workshops that would bring together parliamentarians from both developing countries and from countries operating as banking centers. The goal of this session is to bridge the divide between the ridiculous and the sublime and develop a sensible protocol that could be adopted by affected governments.

Keep in mind that the laundering of corrupt money is not restricted to offshore banking centers or tax havens. By "offshore" we typically refer to countries like the Cayman Islands, Switzerland, Liechtenstein, the Channel Islands, Panama, etc. We know, however, that corrupt money is laundered in a variety of onshore jurisdictions with "not a palm tree in sight" (*The Economist*, 2013). This includes financial centers in locations such as London, New York, Toronto, and Singapore.

As mentioned earlier, the StAR Initiative has recognized the need to focus efforts on the recovery of stolen corrupt assets. StAR "supports international efforts to end safe havens for corrupt funds. StAR works with developing countries and financial centers to prevent the laundering of the proceeds of corruption and to facilitate more systematic and timely return of stolen assets" (StAR, 2013).

Parliamentarians committed to the fight to recover and repatriate stolen corrupt assets are advised to consult with StAR and access their considerable information resources on this topic (Greenberg et al., 2009; Brun et al., 2011). StAR will also provide technical support to parliamentarians in their legitimate efforts to recover stolen assets.

Because of pressure from the OECD, banking centers in locations like Switzerland have been more cooperative in being more transparent and in breaking down the walls of secrecy. Many obstacles remain. These obstacles will be explored in this section.

For off-shore banks, secrecy and confidentiality are their *raison d'être*. The jurisdictions they operate in may not view cooperation with those who are attempting to recover corrupt assets as in their *national interest*. Without the offshore banking business, many of these countries would be severely challenged economically.

Issues associated with dual criminality and double jeopardy create obstacles for the recovery of corrupt assets. Jurisdictions with banking centers may not have laws criminalizing money laundering, thus making prosecutions in those countries difficult to say the least. Bribery of public officials is not an offence per se in many countries. In the same vein, lawyers in these same jurisdictions may argue that if corrupt officials have been convicted or acquitted of corruption charges, they cannot be charged for the laundering of the associated funds.

> Cooperation and information exchange between relevant authorities— those in the country seeking the repatriation of funds, and officials in the country where the corrupt funds have been deposited—are key to successful asset recovery. Success often depends on the thoroughness and quality of preparatory work, which is often significant. In many cases, such work may include providing to facilitate the processing of a mutual legal assistance request, and the forms of, and channels for this stage for formal mutual legal assistance are usually more diverse and flexible. Many of the operational barriers that currently hinder the asset recovery process centre on international cooperation. A lack of trust between jurisdictions may inhibit or delay the provision of mutual legal

assistance, particularly in urgent matters or where jurisdictions have significantly different legal, political, or judicial systems (Open-ended Intergovernmental Working Group on Asset Recovery, 2011).

CONCLUSION

The challenges associated with preventing the laundering of corrupt money, and then recovering those stolen assets that do escape, are daunting and considerable. Parliamentarians are not known to back away from problems or avoid thorny issues. Indeed, parliamentarians have a major role to play in this fight. You are not alone. Organizations like GOPAC, the World Bank Group, StAR, the IMF, FATF, UNODC, the EGMONT Group, Interpol, Transparency International, and others are ready to assist parliamentarians as they tackle the laundering of corrupt money.

The challenge is before us. As U.S. President Obama has said:

> "Change will not come if we wait for some other person or some other time. We are the ones we've been waiting for. We are the change that we seek" (Obama, 2008)

Let us all rise to this challenge.

NOTES

1. By Hon. Roy Cullen, PC, MPA, CA
2. Money Laundering Bulletin, June 2011
3. The Drivers and Dynamics of Illicit Financial Flows from India: 1948–2008; a November 2010 Report from Global Financial Integrity
4. The UNCAC is a landmark, international anti-corruption treaty that offers a comprehensive, global framework for combating corruption. It has been ratified by over 160 countries.
5. According to article 14(1)(b) of the UNCAC, the term "financial intelligence unit" means a national center for the collection, analysis, and dissemination of information regarding potential money-laundering.
6. This survey document is available in English, French, and Spanish on GOPAC's website. The specific English version is at: www.gopacnetwork.org/Docs/ StateOfNationsSurvey2012_EN.docx
7. The FRSBs are as follows: Caribbean Financial Action Task Force (CFATF), Asia-Pacific Group on Money Laundering (APG), Eurasian Group (EAG), Financial Action Task Force on Money Laundering in South America (GAFISUD), Eastern and Southern Africa Anti-Money Laundering Group (ESAAMLG), and Intergovernmental Action.
8. The template legislation is available for civil law at www.imolin.org/pdf/imolin/ ModelLaw-February2007.pdf and for Common Law at www.imolin.org/pdf/ imolin/Model_Provisions_Final.pdf. Additionally, the UNODC Track Legal

Library provides over 50,000 examples of sample legislation, available at www.track.unodc.org/LegalLibrary/Pages/home.aspx.
9. Canadian dollars and US dollars trade roughly at par.
10. I should note that I take some pride in having been very involved myself in the Canadian Parliament in the design and launch of Canada's FIU in 2000! Some might argue that Canada's FIU is the *Rolls Royce* ™ version, but I make no apologies for that!

REFERENCES

Anti-Money Laudering Office of Thailand. (2011). *AMLO Annual Report 2011*. Bangkok.

BBC News. (2010, April). Foreign Firms Pledge Not to Give Bribes in Russia http://news.bbc.co.uk/2/hi/business/8632240.stm

Brun, J.-P., L. Gray, C. Scott, and K. M. Stephenson. (2011). *Asset Recovery Handbook: A Guide for Practitioners*. Washington D.C.

The Economist. (2013, February 16). Offshore Financial Centres: Not a Palm Tree in Sight. p. 8. www.economist.com/news/special-report/21571554-some-onshore-jurisdictions-can-be-laxer-offshore-sort-not-palm-tree-sight

Financial Action Task Force. (2001). FATF 40 + 9 Special Recommendations on Money Laundering & Terrorist Financing www.fatf-gafi.org/media/fatf/documents/FATF%20Standards%20-%2040%20Recommendations%20rc.pdf

Global Financial Integrity. (2010). *The Drivers and Dynamics of Illicit Financial Flows from India: 1948–2008*. Washington D.C. http://india.gfintegrity.org/

Global Financial Integrity. (2013). *Mission & History* www.gfintegrity.org/

Global Organization of Parliamentarians Against Corruption (GOPAC). (2011). *Anti-Money Laundering Action Guide for Parliamentarians*. Ottawa.

Global Organization of Parliamentarians Against Corruption (GOPAC). (2013). *Fifth Global Conference of Parliamentrians Against Corruption: Conference Declaration and Global Task Force Resolutions*. Manila.

Global Organization of Parliamentarians Against Corruption (GOPAC). (n.d.). *Handbook on Parliamentary Ethics and Conduct: A Guide for Parliamentarians* http://gopacnetwork.org/Docs/PEC_Guide_EN.pdf

Greenberg, T.S., L.M. Samuel, W. Grant, and L. Gray. (2009). *Stolen Asset Recovery: A Good Practices Guide for Non-Conviction Baed Asset Forfeiture*. Washington D.C.

Money Laundering Bulletin. (2011, June). *HM Treasury Looks Near and Far.* www.moneylaunderingbulletin.com/legalandregulatory/practicefindings/paper-trail-2247.htm?origin=internalSearch

Obama, Barack. (2008). Super Tuesday Speech. Chicago, Illinois. February 5. http://obamaspeeches.com/E02-Barack-Obama-Super-Tuesday-Chicago-IL-February-5-2008.htm

OECD. (2012). Retrieved from OECD Stat Extracts. Available at: http://stats.oecd.org/.

Open-ended Intergovernmental Working Group on Asset Recovery. (2011, August 25–26). *Towards an Effective Asset Recovery Regime*. Conference of States Parties to the United Nations Convention against Corruption, Vienna.

Stolen Asset Recovery Initiative (StAR). (2013). *About Us*. Retrieved from Stolen Asset Recovery Initiative: The World Bank and UNODC. http://star.worldbank.org/star/

The World Bank, Financial Market Integrity Divisions and International Monetary Fund, Legal Department, Monetary and Financial Systems Department. (2004, July). *Financial Intelligence Units: An Overview.* www.imf.org/external/pubs/ft/FIU/fiu.pdf

Index

For Product Safety Concerns and Information please contact our EU
representative GPSR@taylorandfrancis.com
Taylor & Francis Verlag GmbH, Kaufingerstraße 24, 80331 München, Germany